PEOPLE
BEFORE
THINGS

Change Isn't an End-User Problem

CHRIS LAPING

Illustrations by
Jason S. Rapert

Published by PBT Press, an imprint of People Before Things, LLC
www.peoplebeforethings.co

ISBN 978-0-9973680-0-0
eBook ISBN 978-0-9973680-1-7

Printed in the United States of America
First Edition

Dedicated to

My Grandmothers, Evelyn and Carolyn, who taught me
the true meaning of People Before Things. You are missed.

CONTENTS

PEOPLE BEFORE THINGS

BREATHLESS

"Nothing is so painful to the human mind
as a great and sudden change."

—Mary Shelley

A couple of years ago around New Year's, our family went to Florida and enjoyed a really wonderful vacation at Disney. We bought a three-park pass, which gave us the flexibility to hop from one park to another. While the crowds and lines were really tough to deal with, we had such a memorable time! Our favorite ride was at Hollywood Studios—perhaps you've been on it—Aerosmith's Rock 'n' Roller Coaster. The wait for the attraction was more than two hours so we only got to ride it twice, but we still talk about it like it was yesterday.

Like most roller coasters, there was a weaving line that felt like it was at least three miles long. As we approached the front, we felt the energy of the ride from the happy, excited, and not to mention really scared people jumping into a roller coaster car that was fashioned to look like a stretch limo. I remember staring through the chain-link fence that was positioned at the front of the line and watching the limos line up. While I like roller coasters a lot, I wasn't sure how I felt about what I was witnessing.

You see, the "known for" on this attraction is that the ride starts by immediately launching you from 0 to 57 miles per hour in 2.8 seconds! While the full ride wasn't visible at any point during the waiting process, watching that amazing launch alone built a mound of anticipation for all of us.

Two hours of waiting and visualizing the unknowns led to this moment... we were up. Our family jumped into the limo and, luckily, felt pretty locked in. No fears about safety. Check. I looked over at my then 9-year old daughter and thought, "I'm a terrible dad." She looked back at me, grinning ear to ear, and I realized she didn't agree with me. "I'm a cool Dad!" Check.

The ride started with a slight jerk that faked us out but granted us a few more seconds to collect our thoughts. "This is going to rock! The wait was worth it!" Check. Then, the speakers behind the headrest filled our ears with Steven Tyler, the singer of Aerosmith, counting down... 5... 4... 3... 2... 1. Boom! Just like that, we were fired into a very dark tunnel lit only with strobe lights, Aerosmith blasting over the sound system, and immediate speed consuming our senses!

Here's what I'll tell you about that ride: even though you can see other passengers launch into that dark tunnel before you jump into your limo, it absolutely takes your breath away. Even though you talk about the ride for hours in line, sometimes with strangers who have the same fear and excitement, it takes your breath away. And, even when you've been on the ride before and know exactly what to expect at launch, it takes your breath away.

This experience reminds me why the work of Change Leadership is so important. Change works just like that Rock 'n' Roller Coaster ride. There's long anticipation and build-up, people have a pretty good sense for what's going to happen or have talked to people who do, and in some cases, have already experienced something similar. Yet, time and time again, when something big changes at work, it takes our breath away.

My motivations for writing this book are simple. I've worked in the IT space for 24 years and have seen many companies introduce new technology, the Things, with the hope of building more efficient and effective organizations. (And who can blame them for that—I'm enamored, too. That's why it's my chosen field!) Almost every single one of those projects started with the same promise, "If you invest in this new technology, it will be a game changer." If it's not those exact words from someone in sales, then you often hear from an interested insider, "When we get this new solution, it will free up our people's time to add more value." Here's the punchline: **technology will never do such a thing on its own.**

In fact, if we want to launch a transformation in our organizations, we can only do that by first honoring the human experience, the People, and recognizing how they can dramatically change the outcomes of any

If we want to launch a transformation in our organizations, we can only do that by first honoring the human experience, the People, and recognizing how they can dramatically change the outcomes of any implementation.

implementation. This human experience is the core purpose of my work.

I would love for project teams to feel the joy of making an impact, team members to feel nurtured and supported during a disruptive change, and leaders to feel empowered to act confidently because they have the loyalty and engagement of their people. I believe and want this so much that I'm willing to share some of my biggest failures and personal disappointments throughout my career, as well as the patterns for the approaches that brought the most success.

In full disclosure though, I'm going to provide tough love to leaders because of the hard lessons I've learned during the tenure of my executive career. Fortunately, many leaders I've met and worked with are very self-reflective and willing to improve. So, I trust this information will find a good audience—and my aspiration is that it will positively affect many well-intentioned and hard-working people downstream, who want nothing more than to do a great job and make a difference.

I hope you enjoy this journal of stories and experiences that remind us: if we are going to change our organizations, truly change them, we have to put People Before Things. Always.

CHAPTER 1

FAILURE IS AN OPTION

"Experience is simply the name we give our mistakes."

—Oscar Wilde

SMART ENOUGH, HEALTHY ENOUGH

Patrick Lencioni is a best-selling author and founder of a boutique consultancy called the Table Group. In my opinion, he is the most important thought leader of our generation regarding organizational health and building cohesive teams. His books *Five Dysfunctions of a Team* and *The Advantage* highlight his core belief that to be successful, companies need to be SMART (finance, marketing, strategy, IT, etc.) and HEALTHY (minimal confusion and politics, high morale, high productivity, low turnover). In Pat's experience, companies rarely fail because they aren't SMART enough. As such, he's built a life mission to help organizations get healthier. I couldn't think of a better springboard for the People Before Things movement.

Using Pat's framework, the same could be said about

projects or change initiatives, especially technical ones. For them to be successful, they need to be smart and they need to be healthy. Smart would include all the disciplines of selecting or engineering the right solution, good project management, solid quality assurance, and consistent support and operations. Healthy would include all of the people-related groundwork that needs to be done so team members feel prepared, nurtured, and supported during the changes they will have to adapt to and eventually adopt.

In my experience, failure rarely occurs because project teams aren't smart enough. Rather, projects tend to fail because of people-related issues that cause them to not be healthy enough. This scenario is very common and organizations experience awful consequences as a result. I've experienced failure firsthand, and sharing one of those stories seems like a good place to start.

HEALTHY ISN'T A DECLARATION

We've all worked with someone that annoyed the heck out of us, right? I believe it's only natural that when we spend 8-10 hours a day with people, someone will get under our skin. You know what I'm talking about, don't you? I'm talking about the type of person who just the sight of their face is all you need for a perfectly good day to be ruined. I'll admit it. I've worked with folks like that in my career—and I'm positive I have been "that person" to some of my co-workers!

A number of years ago, I worked with an executive

Failure rarely occurs because project teams
aren't smart enough. Rather, projects tend
to fail because of people-related issues that
cause them to not be healthy enough.

owner who was the arbiter of my team's success on a multi-year, multi-million dollar change initiative. I found his communication style hard to follow and felt more confusion than clarity after conversations with him. However, he was well-regarded by other executives in our organization so I just kept my opinions to myself and hoped no one else shared my feelings.

My team's assignment was to manage a large HR software project that would impact all people, most processes, and some of our technology across the company. It was the type of assignment that I usually relished, but because my favorite guy was the executive owner, I had much trepidation.

As soon as you could spell T-R-O-U-B-L-E, the project was off the tracks. It was time for us to call a project-reset meeting. (Even if you can't relate to working with someone who annoys you, surely you have participated in a meeting like this one? No one is proud or excited to attend.) The objective of the meeting was to gather the key stakeholders for a few hours, opine on our setbacks and obstacles, and build a go-forward plan that everyone felt would succeed. It was an afternoon meeting; I remember it like it was yesterday. We got started on time, and it didn't take long for the team to have crucial conversations about scope creep and underestimated budgets and timelines.

The team identified the root cause for all these issues as the grossly understated impact the technology and process changes were having on our people, which had been a recurring theme since the outset of the project. I was feeling confident that the grassroots leaders of the initiative really understood the issues at hand and didn't need my executive intervention to pace-set their actions.

Just as my confidence started turning into pride because of the team's great action-planning, in walked our hero, 22 minutes late, with a handful of papers and notebooks balancing on the edge of his arms—and a cup of soda hanging from his teeth! It was a grand entrance that absolutely killed the momentum of the discussion. Of course, because he was our executive owner, we respectfully let him settle in and organize his pile of junk.

His settling in took a minute or two, but instead of asking us to carry on, he decided to further interrupt progress and bestow us with a few words of wisdom and inspiration. He cleared his throat, raised his right hand and said, "Team, let me just say... failure is not an option." Just then, I envisioned him sitting in a crowded movie theater watching Apollo 13, stuffing his face with popcorn, and thinking, "Wow, I can't wait to use this line at work one day!" The project team looked stunned. The Project Manager's facial expression said, "Well, there you have it—all of these years spent on certifications, tools, and education, and all I had to do was declare that failure wasn't an option. Who knew?"

WHAT'S AT STAKE?

Here's what I knew during that meeting and actually experienced during that project: failure is absolutely an option! Just declaring, "Failure is not an option," will never help teams avoid failure. It sure didn't help my team. And, what's frustrating about this type of magic wand management is, failure isn't a choice people make. Do you know anyone that gets out of bed in the morning and proclaims, "I want to fail at work today!" I'm guessing not. Rather, failure is often the result of well-intentioned people, who are putting their best efforts forward but experiencing setbacks and obstacles—ones that only leaders can carefully help navigate or mitigate. Therefore, it's imperative leaders lead and provide guidance and support to these smart, hard-working people.

Now, before I go much further, let me touch on my use of the word, "failure." I don't believe the opposite of success is failure. Rather, I believe failure is a step in the process of achieving success. Throughout this book, I purposely avoid using the word because I don't want to give the wrong impression. However, when I use it in a negative context, please know what I really mean is catastrophic failure—the kind that puts companies on the brink of losing everything or significantly impacts the morale of team members.

Let me share some humbling facts that prove (catastrophic) failure is absolutely an option for many teams. According to Gallup, 70% of all change initiatives fail. Harvard Business Review reports that 1 in 6 IT projects have an average cost overrun of 200%. And, Gallup Business Review says that the United States economy loses $50-150 billion per year due to failed IT projects. Wow.

Even if you or I never admitted that we've experienced such dramatic underperformance or failure, we know that from a statistical perspective, many of our colleagues have. I'm guessing that if you talked to anyone who has experienced project failure in their career, the absence of wishing or commanding it away wasn't a lesson learned noted during their look-back meeting.

In my experience, there are some head-slapping, obvious conditions that leaders actually control and prevent projects from hitting a dead end; conditions that promote health. What's amazing is that these conditions don't always require significant, incremental dollars or time to implement. So, how are these head-slapping, obvious conditions created? Quite simply, through Change Leadership. However, as we all know, simple can sometimes be hard. And, as Patrick Lencioni points out, getting healthy is a messy process... so, are you willing to get messy?

CHAPTER 2

CHANGE ISN'T AN
END-USER PROBLEM

"You can't sell it outside if you can't sell it inside."

—Stan Slap

SPEAKING LOUDLY

It was 1996. I was fairly young in my career and taking my first international business trip to Munich, Germany. For weeks leading up to the trip, I went out of my way to educate myself on the German culture and language. I talked to everyone I knew who had traveled to Germany, checked out books from the library, and even watched a German movie that had subtitles. I felt as prepared as I could be. Finally, the time had come to make the big trip, and I was ecstatic when I arrived at the Hotel Splendid in magnificent Munich!

After unpacking and taking inventory of my room, I noticed that an iron was not a standard-issue amenity. I made my way to the front desk and in a typical, arrogant American way (thinking everyone knew at least a little English) said, "Hey, do you have an iron I can get for my room?" The man behind the counter shrugged his shoulders and shook his head. I began to sense he didn't understand me and realized at that moment, that in all my preparation for the trip, I didn't learn how to say the word "iron"—or even how to ask a question like that—in German.

So what did I do? You guessed it. I repeated my question, only this time much louder. Of course, I got the same reaction from the man. Despite my volume, he shrugged his shoulders and shook his head. I moved to indiscernible gestures by grabbing my shirt and making a motion that looked like I was ironing in the air. The conversation ended when the man opened a drawer big enough to hold three pencils and said in very broken English (supported by a frustrated tone), "I have no iron." I was pretty sure he still didn't understand what I needed.

This story illustrates a very basic point. Companies, more specifically leaders, have the tendency to overly rely on communications and training to enable and support change. But, what if their audience understands a different language? A typical corporate cycle looks like this: leaders send out a memo to all team members and ask for compliance on a new, large-scale change initiative. Unfortunately, these leaders receive a high percentage of superficial acceptance that shows up by way of mediocre results. So… they send out another memo—this time from the CEO, because surely a higher title will get everyone's attention. This technique is the corporate equivalent of speaking more loudly in a foreign country.

When this technique doesn't appear to work, the

leaders decide that providing more training will improve compliance. The problem is, training without the proper context and team member alignment can look like the indiscernible gestures I was using in Germany. The outcome is people start looking in pencil drawers for irons, so to speak, which results in guaranteed frustration across the entire organization for leaders, managers, and team members alike.

If we are going to ignite change and truly launch transformation in our organizations, we have to start with the notion that change leadership requires more than speaking loudly. In fact, because we are working with humans and not machines, motivation has to be a part of the equation... and motivation takes time, not decibels.

CHANGE LEADERSHIP DEFINED

I've already made several references to "change leaders." It's natural to wonder how change leaders are different than plain old leaders. In truth, they should be one in the same. Harvard Business Review says that one of the seven skills you need to thrive in the C-suite is change management. I've met many people in the C-suite who have great leadership skills in terms of providing vision and communication and have done an awesome job assembling and managing a talented team. However, they've experienced struggles in leading change because they weren't patient enough and/or their methods for building followership were limited.

As an example, when desired outcomes aren't achieved during the rollout of a new change, you often hear executive

If we are going to ignite change and truly launch transformation in our organizations, we have to start with the notion that change leadership requires more than speaking loudly.

leaders say, "We need to provide better training." Even more common is the approach of writing memos or calling town hall meetings to communicate that team members need to focus more on the desired behavior change and outcome. These approaches put the burden of success squarely on the shoulders of the folks being impacted by the big change. Change leadership takes a different approach. It starts with, "How can I, as a leader, set our people up for success with this new Thing that's coming their way?"

While good change leadership needs project leaders to do their part, it requires enablement by executive leaders prior to the project team lifting a finger on the delivery work. It then requires ongoing nurturing and support (activation) during the implementation phase—which is owned by project leaders, grassroots influencers, and executives. In summary:

Change Leadership =
Enabling + Activating People for Change

Enabling change can significantly impact an organization's preparedness for new Things and is the focus for the second part of this book. I've found three particular conditions have more influence on success than any other: **Alignment, Design** and **Capacity**. I wholeheartedly believe that executive leaders own all three.

I can summarize these three conditions in one sentence:

People need to know why a change is coming and why it is needed (alignment), the change needs to be intuitive and easy to understand (design), and the decks need to be cleared so people can focus on the change (capacity). 99% of the time (I'm leaving the door cracked open for some weird exception), I can trace the project failure I've experienced or observed to people not being on the same page, something being designed very poorly, or people not having enough time to be successful. Mitigating these common issues will make all the difference in the world and will create a great change lubricant.

Once executives grease the skids, it's only then that project leaders are prepared to *activate* people for change, which still by the way requires executive involvement. When people are activated for change, they become loyal and engaged fans who want to help. This is the focus of the third part of the book. In my experiences, I've learned that the four most impactful conditions for activation are **Communications**, **Learning**, **Stakeholder Engagement**, and **Support**. At first glance, this may appear to reinforce straightforward and well-documented tactics around change management. However, there are different ways to think about these four topics—ways that will greatly impact success or failure.

CHAPTER 3

ABSENCE DOESN'T MAKE THE HEART GROW FONDER

*"A leader is one that knows the way,
goes the way, and shows the way."*

—John C. Maxwell

ABSENT EXECUTIVES

Before we jump into the Enablement section of this book, I think it's really important to spend time discussing what it looks like when change leadership is missing—and how team members are impacted by its absence. Based on my own personal experiences and thousands of conversations with project team members and impacted stakeholders, I've concluded that many leaders don't even realize it is often their own lack of engagement and presence during a change cycle that blocks a desired outcome. And, it is this absence that causes well-intentioned, hard-working people (downstream from leaders) to get hurt and demoralized when change initiatives catastrophically fail. I've seen and experienced this defeated feeling myself... many times.

I've also concluded, however, that absence isn't always by choice. In most cases, executives aren't sitting around

Executive absence causes well-intentioned,
hard-working people (downstream from leaders)
to get hurt and demoralized when change
initiatives catastrophically fail.

consciously choosing words and actions that express passive involvement or interest. Whether it's conscious or not, the result is still hurtful and unfortunate. Take these blunders for instance:

First, I was speaking to someone whose husband worked for a public health organization. During a total team meeting, the organization's executives gave their IT department a "Booby Award." I've made mistakes in my career, and I wasn't always the model citizen for how to get things done. Therefore, I understand the angst some folks have with IT. On the other hand, the executives who chose to publicly insult their IT team weren't exactly building an environment that enables change or future success. I'm guessing the recipients of that award didn't feel very supported. Absence.

In another example, I spoke with a former CIO of a company in the business of aerospace engineering. The team members and former CIO himself are some seriously smart engineers (but remember, projects rarely fail because we aren't smart enough)! He shared a story with me about an important technology initiative that had huge change and transformation implications. His team provided the CEO a detailed script for a company town hall meeting with the goal of reinforcing key points related to the project. When it came time to talk about the project, the CEO ditched the script and simply said, "Hey, that ERP project... make sure you pay attention to it!" The team members probably didn't absorb the importance of the project because it was buried underneath inauthentic and ineffective messaging. Absence.

In the final example, I attended a CIO conference that had an audience of well-respected technology leaders representing well-respected companies. Our closing keynote speaker was the President of one of the attending brands. His talk was meant to reassure us the work of IT was vital and, in his case, moving his organization forward. Instead, he bragged to the audience, "My IT guy is here. I don't know exactly what he does, but I know we're spending $30 million a year on technology and innovation." During the Q&A session, one outspoken CIO challenged, "How can you spend $30 million a year and not bother yourself with what your 'IT Guy' is doing?" Right. Absence.

I know all these stories are related to IT, but I share them because of the universality of technology change in organizations today. However, I've seen plenty of examples of non-technical changes, such as the implementation of new policies or corporate reorganizations, which suffer from the same kind of executive absence. The result is almost always the same: a reaction from impacted stakeholders and project team members who inevitably ask, "What planet is that leader living on?" When that occurs, I can confidently confirm, it's game over.

EXECUTIVE OWNERSHIP

There's another nuance to this discussion. It goes beyond behavioral dysfunction of leaders. It's related to structural or procedural constructs and is partially responsible for executive absence. It's commonplace in organizations to label an executive owner of a change initiative as the "executive sponsor." In my opinion, that's where things go wrong. When I think of sponsorship, I mostly think of nonprofit organizations. Sponsorship, especially in that context, means financial contribution; there's usually passive involvement; and it includes the delegation of most decisions. On the other hand, ownership means investment; there's usually active involvement; and it includes being accountable for any and all outcomes. To me, sponsorship vs. ownership is like renting vs. owning.

Project team members desperately need executive leaders to be owners, not sponsors. They need owners to set clear direction and to provide the conditions needed for change success—conditions which team members don't always have enough authority, experience, or context to create. I've sometimes heard executives say, "It's my job to remove roadblocks for the project team." And that's a good start. However, even more useful than removing is *preventing*.

Now we are ready for a healthy discussion on enabling people for change, which includes creating the conditions that *prevent* human-related roadblocks from happening to begin with. Let's get to it!

ENABLING PEOPLE FOR CHANGE

ALIGNMENT

There have been many engagement, retention, and workplace happiness studies completed to highlight what we want at work. Some of us work for money, some of us want growth and development, and some of us want progressive responsibilities. Most of us, however, want to make a difference. When leaders connect people to purpose, they help satisfy that intrinsic need.

Even with all this information at hand, executive leaders tend to focus on the WHAT instead of the WHY. For instance, goals and strategy commonly communicate WHAT needs to be accomplished but often leave out the WHY behind those needs. Fundamentally, it's the underlying purpose (or WHY) that motivates people to get involved in a movement.

Connecting people to purpose also eliminates

confusion. In the absence of clarifying information, team members are left to fill in the blanks. They know completion of a task or project is expected of them, but aren't sure why the work or implemented Thing is truly needed. Therefore, they attach a self-defined laundry list of goals and requirements to the effort—hoping to create clarity and meaning—which may increase the work effort related to their assignment. Even worse, if they get it wrong, rework or throwaway work results. This scenario can be demoralizing and set back an entire organization.

There's nothing more important than connecting people to purpose. It provides meaning; it provides clarity; and it commits a team to the same cause. So why aren't we talking about it?

CHAPTER 4

WE'RE CONFUSED THAT THEY'RE CONFUSED (ALIGNMENT)

"When you're surrounded by people who share a passionate commitment around a common purpose, anything is possible."

—Howard Schultz

WHAT IS ALIGNMENT?

Alignment is a lot like strategy. Everyone says it's important, but it feels like nobody really knows what it means. Some of the most monumental failures in my career came when I was humming along on a project and a fellow team member would tell me, "I don't think we're on the same page." And I'm guessing most of us have heard that dreaded line once or twice. On the other hand, I've experienced tremendous success and joy with teams who felt like we could do no wrong because we were so aligned. The emotional high produced in those moments was amazing. The level of engagement had the whole team hopping out of bed in the morning ready to take on the world. Getting great results and winning is contagious. When everyone is on the same page and perfectly aligned, anything is possible. Anything!

These experiences led me on a journey, about mid-way through my career, to demystify alignment. I wanted to discover why one project might be a huge success from an alignment perspective but another wasn't. I don't profess to have found the Holy Grail, but I did stumble upon one pattern that helped me tremendously. To explain it, I need to take you on an imaginary road trip.

AN IMAGINARY ROAD TRIP

You and I have decided to jump in the car, leave Denver, and head to New York City. With very little conversation, we seem certain that New York City is the right destination. Before we get too far along in our planning, we also decide to include three of our best friends. After all, no road trip is complete without more people in a vehicle than the vehicle is actually intended to hold! Your job is to pick up provisions: simple snacks, water, CDs with '80s music and beef jerky. Yes, beef jerky! My job is to fill up the gas tank with fuel, check the tires, and ensure we have an operable 1987 Chevrolet Chevette ready to go. Yes, a Chevette! We've given our three friends the task of mapping potential routes and deciding amongst themselves the road(s) we will travel.

After a few hours, we all meet at home base with the intention to set out on our journey. The car is ready—full tank of gas and tires at optimal pressure. The provisions are ready—snacks, water, Duran Duran and Devo CDs, and more beef jerky than a small platoon could ever eat! However, our three friends are in a conundrum. It seems they couldn't come to an agreement on the best route for us to take. One route was pretty much a direct path from Denver to New York. A second route took many rural roads to explore America. The third route was a combination of highways and rural roads. While the five of us seemingly decided to take a vacation, we effectively hit a fork in the road (no pun intended) in our planning and execution.

This is where I'd like to interrupt our imaginary road trip. In this story, you and I acted as leaders do in companies all around the world every day. We got aligned on a goal. In this case, it was to take a road trip to New York City. I would argue, though, that our goal got us aligned on the WHAT. Taking a road trip and visiting New York City is WHAT we intended to do. However, our trusted friends were given the task to effectively map a strategy to obtain this goal, and as a result, they presented three sensible routes for us to consider.

Unfortunately, you and I left out the most important part of the discussion—the WHY. It turns out, I was interested in seeing parts of America I had never seen. Back roads would likely have been the best route. You, on the other hand, were interested in seeing the Statue of Liberty, a Broadway production and a slew of other famous attractions because you had never visited New York City. In that case, our best route would have been a straight line across America, minimizing our drive time and maximizing our time in the city. Even though it looked like we were aligned in the beginning, we weren't really aligned at all. Maybe, just maybe, we should've spent more time discussing our motivations and decision before taking any action.

The problem is, we invested money in the provisions and the time of our friends. They were roped in to our goal and actually experienced infighting because they couldn't agree on the right strategy for getting us to New York City. Time, money and relationships were the casualties before we even got on the road and drove a single mile.

It took me years and countless failures before I stumbled upon one pattern for success that was hopefully obvious during our imaginary road trip. True alignment comes from the power of rallying a team to the WHY. You see, we are taught in business school to write goals and build strategy to achieve those goals. However, by their very nature, goals and strategy are very WHAT-oriented. Just like our imaginary road trip, a WHAT goal may lead to many strategic options that just cause confusion and inaction for our teams. However, connecting people to purpose (WHY) provides a powerful filter for strategic and tactical decisions, and more importantly, an engagement mechanism that encourages team members to be more open to change. The research is very clear—people engage in a mission or purpose because they want to make a difference. So, connecting them to the WHY can be transformative.

True alignment comes from
the power of rallying
a team to the

WHY.

A REAL ROAD TRIP

Let me tell you about an unfortunate, real-life road trip which demonstrates the power of WHY, or at least reinforces the weakness of WHAT. A number of years ago, I went offsite with an executive team to do some strategic planning. I have to admit, I was really excited about the trip because I've always been a strategy nerd. We were scheduled for two days in the mountains to get aligned on priorities. I had participated in a countless number of these offsites in my career. There was nothing in particular that signaled this trip was going to be out of the ordinary—until our bus showed up.

The event organizers thought it would provide a bonding opportunity if all the participants rode together. To support this notion, they chartered a bus. Unfortunately, it turned out to be the rustiest, crustiest bus I've ever seen. This thing looked like it was right out of an early '70s episode of Fat Albert and the Gang. I couldn't figure out how this dilapidated machine was going to make it through the mountains, but I suppose it served the purpose because nothing can bring a group of people together like fear and concern!

It only took about 30 minutes after our departure for the bus to break down. At the moment we began our first major ascent, we heard massive grinding noises and the smell of burning oil. Our bus driver was cursing at the Transportation Gods and before we knew it, we were stuck on the side of the road. It turns out that this was just a sign of things to come. To add insult to injury, pictures were circulating in the corporate office. From what I understand, our team back home thought it was funny how all the "high-paid execs" were stranded, and I guess, who could blame them?

Eventually, we got to the mountain resort and jumped right into planning. One of the executives facilitated the discussions. I was impressed with how organized he was. He even prepared mind-maps to ensure we had a productive discussion. I finally recovered from my 1970's Fat Albert and the Gang tour bus hangover and was really digging some of the conversations. Day two was much the same. Lively debate filled the morning and now our facilitator wanted to start summarizing the decisions we made. He asked the participants for assistance, and started acting as a scribe. This was our moment to get aligned on the things we thought were most important and define the rally-cry for our organization. We chose three goals. Drumroll please ... drive traffic, increase sales, and improve profitability.

Now, somewhere along the way in my career, I heard a very helpful adage related to strategy that applies to this story. "If the opposite of your strategy isn't a strategy, then you don't have a strategy!" Using that statement as a guidepost, how many companies out there really had a strategy to decrease traffic, sales, and profitability? I can't think of any. We failed! If our team back home thought it was funny that high-paid execs were stranded on the side of the road because of a broken down bus, I wonder how they felt when those same execs returned from a two-day "boondoggle" (in their eyes) to announce we were going to drive traffic, increase sales, and improve profitability? What's most frustrating to me today about this story is that we had really compelling conversations and lively debate about the needs of our business. However, we articulated them in the most unimpressive and non-clarifying way.

After aligning to the WHAT at the offsite (and defining non-glorious goals at that), the risk of not aligning our team to the WHY became readily apparent. Here's how: we asked the broader team to identify strategies that would help us accomplish the goals we aligned to. Because we hadn't successfully connected people to purpose, the teams met and fought many times over the course of a few weeks, struggling to build a solid plan that met our goals to drive traffic, increase sales, and improve profitability. This outcome was just like our friends in the imaginary road trip who couldn't agree on the best route. In this case, the output was an 11X17 sheet of paper that had approximately 60 strategies captured in 6-point font, which mostly included massive change initiatives that would take years and material investments to accomplish. It was like looking at a roadmap that took 60 different routes to get to the same destination. No focus. No direction. No alignment. No kidding. Even more surprising was the fact that we were confused that they were confused. We felt we provided clarity, but clearly we did not.

Had we shared the underlying WHY of our discussions in the mountains, here's what would have happened: our teams would have understood the opportunities and pain points that were top of mind. As an example, we spent a lot of time at the offsite brainstorming our pricing position in the market. In the months leading to our strategic planning meetings, we received lots of feedback and data from customers, shareholders, and analysts that our product was overpriced. To have pricing power, we needed a more effective cost structure. If we connected people to purpose, we would have shared with the broader team back home that our customers were being hurt with our repeated price increases. This would have created a compelling rally cry to get unnecessary expenses out of the business. That's a much better goal than simply stating, "Improve profitability."

NEVER STOP TALKING ABOUT THE WHY

After many years of working in IT, 14 of them as a Chief Information Officer, I've seen or written hundreds of business cases for technology change initiatives. Some of them made big promises. Some of them were super innovative. Some of them were slam dunks. To be honest, some of them were losers, too. Almost all of them, good or bad, included a formidable WHY in the business case discussion.

Examples included manual pain points to be relieved, product lines to be created, revenue channels to pursue, talent to be developed, and paychecks to be accurately paid. The business cases were filled with promises of work made simpler, processes streamlined, and the mindless and mundane removed. In my opinion, all were worthy WHY statements. What always fascinated me, though, was how so few leaders were talking about the WHY once those initiatives were approved for implementation.

Said another way, the executive owners who chartered the projects tended to rally people around the WHAT. "We're going to roll out an HR system... a new mobile app... a call center solution." Outside of project kick-off meetings, rarely did I hear a WHY statement that sounded like, "We want to make our team members happier by providing more development opportunities, which will be enabled by a new HR system," or any other reference that connected people to purpose. I've encouraged executive owners of technology projects, and sometimes had to be reminded myself, to explore the power of WHY to bring a team together.

If you think about it, not everyone readily knows what an "HR system" is when they first hear their company is going to implement one. It could mean a payroll system; it could mean an onboarding system, and it might even mean an applicant tracking system used for recruitment. Or, it could be all of those things at once. However, if a leader stands up in front of a group and says, "We are working on a new initiative that will help us develop and grow our team members," you could argue there's a clearer message being communicated, which does the double duty of informing people of the initiative *and* motivating them to join the movement.

SIMPLE IS HARD AND
RELATIONSHIPS ARE MESSY

It may seem I'm oversimplifying what it takes to build alignment. However, I recognize getting a team of people to mutually agree to a common WHY can be quite hard. Because there are many messy and complicated people-issues that can arise during a high-conflict debate intended to align a team, there is a tendency to bypass this important work altogether. The approach of avoidance, however, doesn't work—and it's dangerous.

If alignment isn't achieved up front, any change initiative is capable of exposing the slightest organizational dysfunction, which can lead to confusion and rework for many team members. Confusion and rework demoralizes people and keeps them from ever getting to the preference stage of a needed change. That is, a place where a team member says, "I'm so glad we made this change—this is truly a better way to get things done." Without preference, it's hard to achieve meaningful results.

That's why I encourage taking pulse checks to ensure every executive, impacted stakeholder, project team member, and grassroots influencer is reciting the same WHY when working on a change initiative. An initial pulse check should happen at the start of a project but needs to happen again once the project is in motion. If there's misalignment, I immediately hit the pause button. If there's strong alignment, I put a smile on my face and start getting focused on the next important step, design.

ENABLING PEOPLE FOR CHANGE

DESIGN

We explored in alignment how incredibly important it is to connect people to purpose and rally an entire organization around the WHY—the driving need to solve a pain point or seize an opportunity. Change leaders also understand HOW that driving need will be addressed is a great influencer of success. The HOW is formulated in design.

Unfortunately, the business world is littered with examples of leaders who spend valuable time building alignment and then check out during the design process. Either some form of attention deficit kicks in or there is a belief that certain activities are too tactical for executive attention. Whatever the reason, executives should not be absent during this phase. There are many conditions in design that need the attention and support of top leaders.

The #1 enemy of great design and effective execution is complexity. There are some important steps leaders can take to keep design simple. Ultimately, these steps have the same underlying theme: it is essential to perform disciplined mapping of the HOW to the WHY. Also, an engaged and enabling leader will always be on hand to provide clarity and focus when confusion arises during design. This type of leadership helps the implementation team stay on track, and most importantly, ensures compensating measures and workarounds aren't required later because something was poorly designed.

CHAPTER 5

THE EASY BUTTON (DESIGN)

"Design is not just what it looks like and feels like.
Design is how it works."

—Steve Jobs

TRAINING AND COMMUNICATIONS CAN'T SOLVE EVERYTHING

One of my favorite places to get pizza in Denver is a locally-owned restaurant right across the street from Red Robin's corporate headquarters, Mangia Bevi. I used to be a regular there, and since leaving Red Robin, I've frequently craved their thick, salty pizza crust and awesome original creations during my lunch hour. Although I strongly believe they have perfected their pizza recipes, I feel there is one thing they didn't get right—the toilets!

Now, before your imagination takes you to gross images of dirty bathrooms, let me clarify, that there are no cleanliness issues in the restaurant. It's the *design* of the toilets that bothers me. You see, on the bathroom wall, stenciled in paint are the following words, "Please place lid down when finished to activate automatic flush."

Every time I see those words, I start yelling (to myself and anyone who will listen), "If I have to do anything to make the toilet flush, then it isn't automatic! And, if I have to take any action, I'd rather grab a handle than touch part of the seat!"

The thing I find remarkable about this situation is instead of having a plumber replace the toilet with a model that has a better automatic-flush design, the restaurant offers a training and communications solution. The response of posting instructions requires every guest and team member using the bathroom to learn and understand the workaround. And just like that, a simple procedure has been complicated because of poor design. (Don't get me wrong, despite the toilet's design irritation, I still think the restaurant makes one of the best pizzas in Denver.)

As Nir Eyal points out in his book, *Hooked*, "Influencing behavior by reducing the effort required to perform an action is more effective than increasing someone's desire to do it." When a bathroom sign attempts to motivate someone to "activate the automatic flush," it's less effective than if the toilet actually flushed automatically. I continue to make reference to communications and training, and I would never want anyone to think I don't value those activities. They certainly have their place. However, when training and communications are used as techniques to motivate workaround behaviors, I don't think those activities are as useful.

GOOD DESIGN IS MORE
THAN A DECLARATION

Just as I set the stage in Chapter 1 about how declaring, "Failure is not an option," isn't a viable way to ensure future success, let me do the same for the subject of design. I'll always advocate stakeholder feedback as an effective way to build followership and enable change. However, when stakeholders make simple declarations that don't provide tangible or meaningful ways to ensure success, leaders have to guide their teams to a clearer path. Let me explain more.

Design can be a frustrating subject. I've learned there are more armchair quarterbacks in the world of design than just about any other functional area in IT. No matter what type of technology I've implemented over the years, someone had an opinion. Predictably, the opinion was a universal declaration that sounded like, "The solution needs to be intuitive and easy to use," as if engineers and creative types make it their goal to produce something that doesn't make sense and is hard to use.

I believe, as leaders, we have an opportunity to impact our organizations with thoughtful design. It starts with recognizing that declaring, "This 'new thing' needs to be intuitive and easy to use," will never enable a better outcome. More importantly, when something is not getting the adoption we want due to complexity, we need to acknowledge that training and communications aren't always the best way to solve the problem, especially if it's nothing more than a workaround.

Leaders need to recognize that declaring, "This 'new Thing' needs to be intuitive and easy to use," will never enable a better outcome.

There have been times in my career when I implemented systems that were embarrassingly hard to use. The executive owners of those projects insisted additional training and communications would help with the related adoption issues. To me, this response was a lot like painting instructions on the wall for a toilet that doesn't work as expected. I've noticed this common reaction isn't limited to technology either. Whether it's a new benefit plan from HR, travel and entertainment policy from Accounting, or dress code from Operations, there is an inordinate tendency during deployment to lean on talking points and training materials to make sense of things poorly designed or not thought out.

In my opinion, design is absolutely a function of leadership rather than a milestone solely delegated to working teams. This is a point many leaders will argue I'm sure, but when I ask who made the decision to purchase a new technology product to begin with or whose name is on the purchase order, their fingers inevitably point back to themselves. I've always believed executives interested in enabling change will accept ownership and willingly play a key role in the design process. The often-used and most relevant success story supporting this belief was Steve Jobs, who made design a primary differentiator for one of the most well-known companies in the world, Apple.

So how can leaders be active and involved owners of a solid design process? I believe there is a natural order of supporting steps that produce intuitive and easy-to-use solutions, which require less training and communication backstops to be successful.

Summarizing these steps: 1) encourage **human-centered design** to *identify* the most important features needed to respond to the WHY; 2) embrace a **"less is more"** philosophy to *implement* the most important features from the human-centered design work and nothing more; 3) and **always share what's next** on the solution roadmap with impacted stakeholders to *communicate* what future features may be included. Let's explore these steps in more detail.

HUMAN-CENTERED DESIGN

It was the beginning of 2011 and iPads were taking the world by storm. As Red Robin's Chief Information Officer and Senior Vice President of Business Transformation, I had plenty of reasons to be interested in Apple's new product. After all, Red Robin had 26,000 team members, 87% of them millennials, and the early data indicated a higher adoption rate of the new tablets by this target demographic.

My core responsibility as the CIO was to integrate emerging technology relevant to the business that could impact the company's top or bottom line. My core responsibility as the SVP of Business Transformation was to ignite change within our entire restaurant workforce, which included a new generation of team members who had different work preferences and learning styles. Wearing both hats, it was a high priority to investigate the possibilities of tablets in the restaurants.

Two of my teams, Learning and Development and IT, were collaboratively looking at technology alternatives to deliver restaurant training. The old training was nothing more than a series of physical manuals, which were expensive to keep up-to-date and relied on analog means to teach a digital generation. Because the manuals weren't relevant enough, team members weren't learning or retaining core concepts; this was a huge challenge for a brand that was experiencing 80+% turnover. It didn't take long for us to realize iPads might be an awesome alternative to consider.

Our Learning and Development team approached the project utilizing a human-centered design technique called DACUM (Developing a Curriculum). In a nutshell, the process locks a group of representative end-users of training into a room with a facilitator to identify, in the view of the end-users, what skills need to be learned and mastered the most if they are going to be successful in their day-to-day jobs.

The output of these sessions includes an inventory of skills that require curriculum development. More importantly, an inventory of "not needed" skills is identified and put on a potential stop-doing list; this list included skills we were actively reinforcing in our current training program. While the DACUM process is focused specifically on the development of curriculum, human-centered design takes the same approach for the development of technology solutions. For any respective area requiring a new solution, it's about asking a representative group of end-users, "If you were in the driver's seat for something new, what would it look like? If you were solving this problem, how would you solve it?" No preconceived solutions or approaches are introduced during these discussions.

By putting the end-users in the center of design, we got a much better view of their specific needs and were able to cull useless information that got in the way of learning the most important skills. An interesting aside is we also realized during the DACUM process team members didn't feel like they were getting enough practice time on the new skills needed to succeed. We knew the time savings gained from culling useless information could be used to provide more effective ways to practice, and hone team member skills. From this process, the idea was born to build iPad-based game simulations, which enabled repetition and practice but was also perceived by the team members as relevant, innovative and fun.

For most leaders, *facilitating* a human-centered design session doesn't seem like a task they should be doing. I agree. In fact, I never facilitated one human-centered design session at Red Robin (though I attended many). However, two things are required from a leader to *enable* human-centered design: first, a leader has to exercise patience and encourage the project team to pull representative end-users into a room to talk about their needs. As sensible as that approach may seem, I've heard leaders express time and time again, "We just can't take team members away from their day job to work on this project." Or, "If we make sure the solution is intuitive and easy-to-use, everyone will be fine." These kinds of statements obviously kill human-centered design before it ever gets started, are shortsighted, and will likely lead to rework and resistance later.

Second, a leader has to demonstrate *courage* and let end-users (customers or internal stakeholders) drive the kind of solution they need to properly support their work. Sometimes, this approach can produce an outcome or design contrary to the leader's intuition or intention, and it takes courage to accept this conclusion. I've also seen, on occasion, end-users question faulty assumptions and the WHY they were asked (by leaders) to rally around. This resulted in a pause or reconsideration of the project. To me, those are still positive outcomes because they demonstrate a leader's willingness to listen and focus on people's needs rather than force-feed some new Thing.

LESS IS MORE

After representative end-users provide feedback about what is really needed to solve a problem or seize an opportunity, leaders will most likely conclude people have fairly simple, addressable needs. The goal is to never lose sight of this conclusion. I acknowledge, however, I myself have prescribed some overly complex solutions for simple needs. As a result, one thing I've learned in my career is that complexity is the #1 enemy of great design and execution. When I was successful, it was because I kept the solution lightweight and mapped all features directly to the WHY. In a way, this approach reminds me of a key lesson we can learn from mobile apps.

When mobile apps were new on the scene, I found myself wondering why most people (including me) loved them so much. Believe it or not, I found my answer standing at the toaster one morning making breakfast. It occurred to me that a mobile app is just like my toaster—a single-purpose device. When I want to toast something, I use a toaster. If I want to reheat a burrito from yesterday's lunch, I'm out of luck. That's what I use a microwave for... it's great for re-heating my burrito, but if I want to brew a pot of coffee, then once again, I'm out of luck.

And, the list goes on and on. An electric toothbrush cleans my teeth. A vacuum cleaner sucks up the junk. A lawn mower cuts the grass. We live in a world of single-purpose devices, and most people like it that way. Mobile apps are digital versions of single-purpose devices. They are generally engineered to perform a function or two at most. You want to manage a to-do list? Download Wunderlist. You want to post photos? Download Instagram. You want to get directions? Download Waze.

This is so contrary to the traditional, enterprise IT systems, which act as Swiss Army Knives and provide different functionality all-in-one. People are forced to click through ten screens to get to the one thing that matters the most. Then, when they get there, the one thing that matters the most didn't really function the way they actually needed it to. (Can you say, "Human-centered design?")

Leaders enable change when they encourage project teams to design to the WHY and nothing more. It's actually surprising how that single design principle culls out tons of features and functions people don't actually care about, which mitigates change activation nightmares later down the road. If you're implementing new technology, turn off all the extras. In fact, don't even buy them if you have a choice. If you're implementing a new policy or process, remove all the rules or steps that don't directly map to the WHY. Showing the team you're interested in making their lives easier is a great way to put People Before Things.

ALWAYS SHARE WHAT'S NEXT

I have to be honest about the advice I just gave regarding the less is more concept: when I've been most disciplined about sticking to this principle, I've been "punched in the throat" by people who felt their needs weren't being considered. Even when I offered rational reasons as to why their needs weren't aligned with the collective organization or the driving WHY, feelings were hurt and engagement was lost. Nothing was gained. In other cases, I could rationally demonstrate the solution *was* aligned to their needs, but team members would explain it woefully missed the mark, and they needed more. In either scenario, I learned one design tactic that had a positive impact—always share what's next.

To build followership, leaders have to provide line-of-sight visibility to all team members about what's important now and how that fits into what's important in the future. Leaders do it all the time, but usually in the context of goals and strategy. Emulating this behavior for disruptive change is just as important. It can be as simple as, "Here's where we are today, and here's where we intend to be in the next 6-12 months. What do you think?" It can also include a more detailed product roadmap outlining future enhancements. I've always believed progress is the most important metric of success in any organization. People will mostly pardon the dust, as long as positive progress continues to be made.

However, if people get the impression some disruptive change is being imposed on them and the related conditions will never evolve or improve, they will resist with all their might. This happens a lot in politics and our government. Once a law is enacted, it is extremely difficult to amend in the future. People know this. Therefore, politicians filibuster and endlessly debate to block the change. The same is true, in particular, with technology implementations. If team members get the impression they're stuck with a never-evolving, rigid and complex system, it is a recipe for disaster. They will absolutely push back and resist.

As I said earlier, design can be challenging. However, design is where the rubber hits the road between vision and execution, and it deserves the attention and experience of executive leadership.

Design clarity provides another useful and important benefit—it helps a leader more precisely define the time required to properly adopt a change. And as we will soon find out, nothing is more valuable than time.

ENABLING PEOPLE FOR CHANGE

CAPACITY

We live in a world that promotes and celebrates busyness. Think about it. How many times have you heard co-workers brag, "During my day off, I ran 20 miles!" Or, what about the people who repeatedly boast about how little sleep they get because they are so busy? While on the surface, busy looks like an effective metric for productivity and success, it can do more harm than good—yet it is consistently and positively reinforced in society.

In most cases, people feel pressure to multitask in order to meet their work and leisure commitments. However, studies show that (for the majority of us) our brains are actually incapable of multitasking, especially when it comes to the types of activities required of knowledge workers. In addition, when people don't have time to focus, it is hard to find the discretionary effort required to learn about and adopt new changes. As a result, many opportunities and returns on investments are never realized.

The most successful leaders connect people to purpose, provide great clarity and focus during design, AND ensure their team has the time required to do the job right. Otherwise, frenetic environments promoting the trivial many will result in overwhelmed team members who resist change and hate going to work.

CHAPTER 6

TEN POUNDS OF CRAP IN A ONE-POUND BAG (CAPACITY)

"If you don't have time to do it right,
when will you have time to do it over?"

—John Wooden

DARLEY & BATSON

In 1973, Princeton psychologists John Darley and Daniel Batson conducted an experiment with campus seminarians preparing for ministry. A portion of the involved students were asked to give a talk on the Good Samaritan and assigned a sermon time and location. When the students arrived at their prescribed meeting place however, they were told the location was changed last minute—to the other side of Princeton's campus. This message was delivered with three very different time pressures. One group of students was told they had more than enough time to get to the other side; one group was told they had just enough time; and the last group was told they were already late.

Along the path, the psychologists introduced a distraction. They arranged for an actor to lie on a sidewalk between the two locations. As seminarians approached the man, he asked for assistance. While it wasn't clear if the man was drunk, a victim of violence or having a medical situation, he clearly needed help. Here is what Darley and Batson found: for the students who were told they had plenty of time to get to the new sermon location, 63% of them stopped and offered the man assistance; for the students who were told they had just enough time, 45% of them stopped; and for the students who were told they were already late, only 10% of them stopped to help.

The real punch line of this experiment is that the psychologists screened all potential seminarian subjects, ensuring they had similar values and personalities. So, it turns out, even when people are aligned to a cause, time constraints have a huge impact on their willingness to get involved.

WHY DON'T WE HAVE TIME?

At one point in my career, I worked with an executive who used to say, "Ten pounds of crap in a one-pound bag." Her intention in using this expression was simple. In her view, there was no additional capacity in the company to take on more work. Very often, I found myself agreeing with her. What I found startling though was that all of the other executives in the room agreed with her, too.

This circumstance left me completely bewildered and amazed. If we all felt the organization had too much going on and there wasn't enough focus, wasn't it our jobs to fix that problem? Certainly, as leaders, we must have caused this state of affairs with our lack of prioritization or our

Even when people are aligned to a cause,
time constraints have a huge impact on
their willingness to get involved.

desire to accomplish more than we could at any one time. Instead, the executives often acted as if this overflow of tasks was something our team members actually wanted or caused themselves.

Someone on the executive team might ask, "Why is everyone so busy? What are they working on?" If one executive tried to answer the question with a laundry list of projects and tasks, another executive might say, "Everyone says they're so busy, but when I walk around the building at 5:05 P.M., nobody's here!" Honest to God, these are actual phrases I have heard in relation to capacity and priorities, and I've heard similar comments across many companies and leadership teams.

Based on these experiences, I can't help but wonder—do we, as executives, really think people are preoccupying themselves with a lot of busy work, and demanding everything needs to be done right now? Do we believe by making comments about our team members not putting in discretionary effort when workloads are (or at least feel) overwhelming, the issue will be fixed; will comments such as that magically ignite a drive within our teams to work more hours and on more tasks? And, if we do believe those things, do we think all the neuroscience findings about multitasking don't apply to our own work environment?

In our day-to-day lives, we've watched the world rapidly devolve to a multitasking work engine that has progressively become more and more interrupting. There's hardly a minute or even a second to waste; there is a constant demand to do more with less. While boosting productivity has been a noble goal since the inception of the Industrial Revolution, the problem is, it sometimes puts profits in front of people. And, what's tough about this notion, team members sense and know this reality. Said another way, people are highly aware of matters related to time and are constantly feeling the pressure of unrealistic expectations. Many employees regularly skip their lunch break and give that time to their employer, despite wellness statistics that say this is an unhealthy behavior. I've heard a story about a project manager needing steroid shots to treat stress-induced pain in her shoulder. And we've all worked with team members that come into work despite being sick. These are all signs that our teams feel the pressure of time.

I've experienced projects that had really strong organizational alignment because people had line-of-sight visibility to WHY those projects were needed. In some of those experiences, the new Things being implemented were actually designed really, really well, too. That is, end users were involved in the design process and communicated during the test period, "Wow, this is so easy to use and it's going to make my job easier... I can't wait for it to be implemented!" And, even with that kind of solid design and organizational alignment, I've seen complete implosions during the deployment phase of a needed change; the ultimate users just wouldn't adopt the solution. One pattern existed in all those implosions. People were up to their noses in day-to-day tasks and hardly had a moment to breathe, much less dedicate 5-10 hours a week for several weeks to learn something new.

This situation is sometimes referred to as task saturation. Exacerbating the issues of task saturation in the workplace is the fact that our modern world has filled people's personal lives with many things they have to learn and adopt. I think of working parents who might be focused on a new school year and the transition activities of their children, like online assignment/grading and volunteer tools that need to be learned. Then, there are people who might be helping a sick parent or friend and are forced to learn new medical terms, about medications, care worker names, and how to use medical devices. Whatever the case may be, just hoping people will find the additional time needed to adapt to and adopt a workplace change above a normal 40-hour work week doesn't set team members up for success.

So, now that we've adequately defined the time challenge, how can change leaders enable their people and organizations for success? In my experience, there are really only two logical solutions: 1) Ensure people are focused only on the critical elements ("**The Vital Few**") of the business and nothing more; and/or 2) **Accommodate the needed time** (i.e. backfills, schedule time) to adapt to and adopt a new change.

THE VITAL FEW

I once attended an offsite meeting with leaders of a fairly large company to talk about strategic priorities for an upcoming year. Part of the agenda included a discussion about the current challenges and opportunities that needed action planning, which was a critical step should the group want to be successful meeting their goals. Leader after leader expressed how too many competing priorities were causing confusion and angst across the organization and that they couldn't think about adding any more work for the New Year.

I felt the same way and expressed my personal opinion on the matter. The CEO spoke up and sternly said, "We've got to be able to walk and chew gum at the same time. We can't afford to stop our business to play catch-up in the marketplace."

On one hand, I completely agreed with him—the competitors were not going to sit around waiting for us to implement new Things that would help us take market share. On the other hand, I didn't understand why we, the executive leaders, weren't getting really clear on the things that mattered the most and ensuring our people's time and focus were placed only on those priorities.

If I were given back that moment in time, I might have used a break to quickly catch up with the CEO and remind him that the topic of capacity doesn't require an all or none approach. I don't think the leaders in the room expected he would choose to just walk or just chew gum. Rather, I think the leaders in the room wanted to hold off on a few chews of the gum while we focused on taking a few crucial steps.

In mathematics, the theory of optimization basically says one thing will come at the cost of another. There is a technique called linear programming, which is used to find the best solution with limited resources to maximize profit or minimize cost. The key to both points is when you manipulate one variable it changes the impact of other variables. This isn't an assumption, it is MATH! Yet, when allocating their people's time to work efforts, leaders often ignore it. And unfortunately, this leadership approach often results in over-extended and exhausted team members. Chip Heath, author of the book *Switch* points out, "Change is hard because people wear themselves out... what looks like laziness is often exhaustion."

There's another occurrence in organizations that leaders need to be conscious of and which contributes to the growing laundry list of to-dos. Like a snowball rolling down a hill, getting larger and larger as it does, leaders have the tendency to add their own priorities to company goals as they cascade them to team members. As an example, a CEO might communicate three important goals to her direct reports—goals that must be accomplished in the near future. Her direct reports, in turn, meet with their teams to share the CEO's goals, but might also add a goal or two they think is important. Now, everyone is working on up to five goals. And the next level of management does the same. This cycle repeats itself over and over again to the point of leaders sitting around asking, "How did the vital few become the trivial many? And why is everyone so busy?"

As Greg McKeown brilliantly points out in his book *Essentialism*, "The word *priority* came into the English language in the 1400s. It was singular. It meant the very first or prior thing. It stayed singular for the next five hundred years. Only in the 1900s did we pluralize the term and start talking about *priorities*. Illogically, we reasoned that by changing the word we could bend reality."

ACCOMMODATE THE NEEDED TIME

Maybe you and other leaders in your organization feel your teams are already working on (only) the highest priority projects and tasks (the Vital Few). Yet, you keep hearing people say they just can't keep up, let alone take on any new work. So, how can you really know it's time to put less crap in a bag? One way to know is by completing a time and motion study. Leaders usually see this practice as an overwhelming task, unless they happen to work in manufacturing or have strong industrial engineering support in their business. While it's absolutely the best way to understand what is required of people to manage their jobs effectively from a time perspective, I recognize very few companies and leaders are willing to take this step.

In lieu of doing this kind of industrial engineering work, leaders can perform an easy, high-level analysis of the incremental effort required by a new change initiative. I call the outcome the Capacity Index, which is detailed in *The Nitty Gritty* chapter at the end of this book. The Capacity Index can be used as a relative measure to understand how heavy (or light) a change will be from a time commitment standpoint—relative to other changes being implemented in the organization. This information is pretty powerful at an individual change initiative level, but even more helpful at a portfolio level.

A given leader may only be responsible for pushing a major change or two throughout the course of a year.

However, the impacted team members may be receiving dozens of changes during the same period of time from other leaders. Having a macro view of those changes and being able to provide a monthly Capacity Index roll-up will help prepare for the times of year which may be more heavily weighted with change than others. When implementing a new Thing is vital to the business, it may make sense to clear the decks of other new Things to ensure the total team is doing a great job with the vital one.

I will say it again—this approach doesn't have to be an all or none proposition. However, the closer you get to offsetting the time and effort required to take on a new change, the more likely you will achieve your expected outcome(s).

Another option outside of minimizing the number of large changes you push at any one time is to augment/offset the labor required to properly absorb a new change. As an example, if you're rolling out a new payroll system, it may make sense to add temporary payroll staff to the team to help process the same number of paychecks.

Let's say your team typically processes 10,000 payroll checks with five team members. Since those five folks are learning how to efficiently and effectively interact with a new system, you may want to add the temporary labor of two to three additional people. While there will be a short-term cost associated with such an action, you will offset the risks associated with team members not having the appropriate amount of time to learn the new system and process issues that may arise. Most importantly, you will be indirectly communicating to your payroll team that you care about them and want them to feel supported during such a disruptive change.

That's what enabling people for change and change leadership is all about. It's about taking action in the best interest of your team. And it's about putting their needs in front of unrealistic expectations of discretionary (and heroic) effort.

CHAPTER 7

IT'S GO TIME!

"Motivation is the art of getting people to do what
you want them to do because they want to do it."

—Dwight D. Eisenhower

STICKING WITH THE TREATMENT

A few years ago, I was training for a big run in the
mountains—the Colorado Relay. This relay race covers
200 miles and encompasses 12,000 feet of elevation change
with a team of ten runners. I'd participated in the event
the previous two years; by the third year, I was finally
getting smart about the type of training required to be
properly prepared. Specifically, I learned from the other
runs that simply hitting the pavement and logging daily
miles wouldn't set me up for success. You see, a significant
obstacle standing in my way was the amount of pain and
discomfort I felt during and after my runs.

I decided to solicit the help of a chiropractor, one who
was an experienced runner and cyclist himself. After an
extensive conversation, he did some poking and prodding
and then ordered x-rays to determine my overall condition.

A week later, I returned to my chiropractor's office to hear his comprehensive assessment of my structural health. He pulled a chair up close, looked me in the eye and said, "You have some significant issues we need to address. And here's the thing, Chris... *pain is the last thing that shows up, and it's the first thing that goes away.* You waited too long to have your condition addressed. As such, treatment is going to take time and patience." He paused and very sternly told me, "I need you to stick with the treatment plan. In a few weeks, you'll start to feel better, but you need to remember the pain is the first thing that goes away. You've got to stay dedicated so we can address the source issues and meet your long-term goals."

This advice had a significant impact on my running performance that year and will stay with me for life. *"Pain is the last thing that shows up, and it's the first thing that goes away."* I've found it applies to many situations unrelated to physical health, too—such as change leadership and organizational health.

As an example, if executives apply the advice about enabling change through **Alignment**, **Design**, and **Capacity**, the pain of initiating a big organizational change might go away. An executive might see a lot of head nodding and might even hear stakeholders say, "I'm excited!" As such, it will be very tempting to ditch the "treatment plan" and think all is well. However, like my Colorado Relay training experience, executive leaders need to stay dedicated to the total change leadership treatment plan if they want to see impactful, long-term results. This requires not only enabling people for change up front, it requires activating people during key phases of the implementation. And sometimes, that can take a lot more time and patience than executives are willing to give to "a project." Believe me, whether they communicate it to you or not, your project teams and stakeholders need your involvement.

SO NOW WHAT?

Execution is where the responsibility and conversation of change leadership starts to include project leaders and grassroots influencers. In concert, all three groups (executives, project leaders and grassroots influencers) have to work together to activate people for change. To me, activation means motivation; it means engagement; and it means building followership. When this happens, it results in stakeholders acting as loyal and engaged "fans" who want to help and are more forgiving of hiccups. This type of working environment is very powerful and will save you from months of rework, failed implementations, and perhaps even turnover.

Just as we discussed with enabling people for change, there are conditions that should be created to help activate involved and impacted stakeholders. Before we cover those conditions however, we should take a moment to address those difficult co-workers or customers that must adopt the change you're pushing. You know the ones, right? Those people that just refuse to change...

WHY WON'T THEY JUST CHANGE?

I don't believe people are born lazy or obstinate. Even though science has proven that human beings (and most animals) will minimize their level of effort to get the maximum return, I don't see that as a weakness; it's just biology. None of us deserve to be judged for that kind of behavior. That said, we've all noticed people in the workplace who don't appear to be cooperating or complying with the grand corporate plan—frankly, they appear to be making no effort at all. Let's be real. *No* effort is different than minimal effort.

Over the years, I've kept a mental ledger of such behavior, especially when my teams were driving a large change and adoption was at risk. I had an intellectual curiosity to understand why certain people in the broader organization were not behaving as expected. While seeking out this knowledge, I turned to frameworks like the Change Curve to provide clarity. To be honest, I felt there had to be an easier way to explain why people were not behaving or responding as planned. And believe it or not, I found my answer in the world of marketing.

Based on my learnings but applied to change, it turns out it's pretty simple. When something new is introduced, people may not behave as expected because of one of three reasons: 1) They aren't *aware* of the change; 2) They don't *understand* how to be successful with the change; and/or 3) They don't *care* about the change.

First, it's quite possible that people just don't have

Every individual involved in leading
and receiving "the change" must move
through these states:

PREFERENCE

"I am ready to
adopt the change!"

UNDERSTANDING

"I have the skills I need
to adapt to the change."

AWARENESS

"I know about the change."

awareness that change is coming. I always found it embarrassing when this circumstance happened under my leadership, but sometimes it did. As much as I considered myself a strong communicator, there were times when I flat out forgot to mention to my team or a group of unsuspecting stakeholders that some type of change was coming their way. Or, I may have communicated something, but it got completely lost during the organizational cascading process. I've seen other leaders make the same mistakes. Obviously, when the impacted stakeholders had no knowledge of something, they took no action. Duh!

This makes me think back to the Red Robin days when we ambitiously planned to roll out one of the most relevant and profitable loyalty programs in the casual dining industry, Red Robin Royalty. Today, the program has over five million members and is quite successful. It wasn't always smooth waters though—work that began in earnest in 2008 took until 2011 to design, test, and deploy.

During the test roll out, we really wanted team members to talk about the new program with our guests. However, when we walked into some of our test restaurants a few months after the pilot started, we found some servers and bartenders didn't mention the program at all. It turned out that those team members weren't employed at Red Robin when the initial, test roll out and training occurred. We hadn't operationalized the communications or learning— as new team members were onboarded, they received only loose and indirect information about the program. Therefore, they had little or no awareness, and subsequently,

PEOPLE BEFORE THINGS

weren't talking about it with their guests.

Second, even when team members have awareness, there's typically a group of people who don't quite have an *understanding* of how to be successful when a new change is rolled out. Yes, these folks may have seen the memo announcing the importance of everyone's compliance to the new change, and may have even been told WHY the change was important. However, they may lack the essential skills required to actually do what they were told. This situation is a little harder to detect because people aren't always forthcoming when they don't understand something or feel they are deficient.

Reflecting on the Red Robin Royalty program example, we learned from the test to be more directive and clear about our expectations. We also ensured that team members learned about the program during their onboarding and new-hire process. Even with those improvements, we still had some team members who weren't mentioning the program to their guests. After further analyzing the problem and talking to many team members, we learned that the servers didn't necessarily have the needed skills to market and sell non-food items. As a result, they didn't talk about the program most of the time because talking about it actually made them feel quite awkward. In this case, they were fully aware, but it was their lack of understanding blocking adoption.

Finally, I've been in situations where people clearly have awareness of the expectations and an understanding of the skills needed to succeed, yet they continue to ignore the change. When this happens, you have a more challenging condition to overcome. These people may not actually care; said another way, they most likely lack *preference* for the change.

Returning to the loyalty program case study, we eventually built up the skills of our servers so they could market and sell non-food items to guests. We even helped team members script exciting ways to talk about the benefits of the program, which made them feel less awkward. As a result, servers started doing a better job marketing the program up front in the guest experience. However, despite this "win" we found that some servers weren't actually asking guests for their loyalty cards at the end of the meal. (Talk about hitting your head up against a wall just to make a program work!) While trying to identify the root cause of this behavior, one team member was honest and admitted, "When guests use their loyalty card, they get a discounted meal. Since the guest tips on the discounted total, my income potential is impacted." Clearly, the server didn't prefer the loyalty program because it was messing with her variable rewards. Therefore, she wasn't complying with the new standard operating procedures.

ACTIVATE!

The key point is this: change leadership requires a diverse and comprehensive set of conditions to activate people for change—and these conditions must achieve the outcomes of awareness, understanding and preference. As an example, written communications may help achieve high-level awareness about a coming change, but how can a person learn the necessary skills required to be successful with a disruptive change from a memo (understanding)? And, even if you were brilliant enough to achieve that impossible task, I've never read a memo that on its own accord caused me to immediately jump up and cheer, "Hallelujah, I'm so glad this change is coming—I want it now!" (preference).

Therefore, we as leaders need to be more intentional than just writing memos to activate people for change. Instead, we need to be like those evil marketing geniuses who convert us from a state of not knowing or caring to a state of, "Oh my God, I've just gotta have it!" To do this, we have to carefully and patiently move our team members from awareness to understanding to preference to gain followership and motivate human behavior. After all, the leader got to go through the same cycle when she was deciding to push the change initiative to begin with.

I know this approach might seem overwhelming for leaders who have an incommensurable and varied audience of stakeholder groups. Don't be discouraged. These outcomes can be achieved with a set of conditions that are targeted to reach people where they are: **Communications**, **Learning**, **Stakeholder Engagement**, and **Support**. Without these conditions, change adoption is at risk. With them, change is activated. And even better, when it occurs consistently, you have armed your company with the best weapon on any side of the Mississippi River—you've ignited a culture of change!

ACTIVATING PEOPLE FOR CHANGE

COMMUNICATIONS

No one aspires to be a poor communicator, and just about everyone thinks they're an attentive listener. However, in most organizations, leaders and team members alike believe their work environment is cluttered with ineffective communications. Why is that? There are countless books and development offerings that focus on the topic. In addition, tools like social networking, texting, and collaborative team sites have been added to the mix of delivery options. Even so, we still read and hear about communication failures daily.

Perhaps all of these methods and tools ignore the real root causes and, until they're addressed, communications might not be the panacea we think it is. In fact, relying on communications to drive change adoption just might be the most over-prescribed painkiller in Corporate America. Considering the various communication preferences people have and the diverse styles in which leaders deliver a message, maybe our expectations for communications as a change tactic should be much, much lower.

Change leadership is focused on building follow-ership, and followership happens when impacted stakeholders graduate from awareness to under-standing to preference. Although communications are an important part of change delivery, they should be used to do nothing more than create awareness.

CHAPTER 8

THIS AIN'T A BOX OF DONUTS (COMMUNICATIONS)

"The more elaborate our means of communication,
the less we communicate."

–Joseph Priestley

TIMES HAVE CHANGED

A few years ago, I sat in a software sales pitch meeting for an up and coming company, which has since become an industry leader. The sales rep was an energetic guy with strong presentation skills and a knack for holding my interest. My team met with him several times, and I could sense he felt we were ready to buy at any given moment. He was anxious to close the deal.

During the meeting, he walked through a sales-closing PowerPoint deck intended to imbue our confidence and persuade us to finalize our decision. His presentation started nicely and was well rehearsed. One of the first few slides really got my attention. So much so, I unfortunately started to tune him out.

The slide was labeled *Times Have Changed* and included the covers of five Time Magazine issues. One magazine cover highlighted how people were disenchanted with the government; another headlined rising fuel prices; a third cover mentioned the recession; and the last two spotlighted diplomacy issues in Iran and the volatility of the stock market. In a perfectly timed punch line the sales rep said, "This is what was going on in the world when our competitor developed the other solution you are considering. These magazine covers are from the 1970's—the other solution is old, outdated and shouldn't be in your consideration set!" I officially stopped listening, but not because I was ready to buy.

Inside my head, I thought, "What? 1970's? These are the exact things we are struggling with in our generation! How can this be?" I became obsessed with this slide. Here we were 40 years later experiencing the same socio-political issues. Since that meeting, I've thought about those magazine covers a lot, and here's what I've resolved: as a society, we must be really good at making problems go away but not effective at actually solving them. Said another way, we treat the symptoms with "painkillers" but don't address the underlying, root cause.

If we were to do the same thing in the business world and look at Harvard Business Review or BusinessWeek covers from 40 years ago, would we see the same sort of thing? Would we see companies struggling with a lot of the same issues we experience in our organizations today? I think we would. Surely, one of those struggles would be communications. And while the business world has tried to make communication problems go away with

While the business world has tried to make communication problems go away with painkilling technologies like email, collaboration sites, texting, smartphones, etc., the truth is, we haven't treated the underlying root cause.

painkilling technologies like email, collaboration sites, texting, smartphones, etc., the truth is, we haven't treated the underlying root cause. The communication vehicle or lack thereof isn't the issue—the approach is.

While I don't purport to have a solution for every last communication problem, it seems to me there's an opportunity to address a few root causes that apply to pushing change. What I've learned (the hard way) about communications is that they must: 1) Come from **an important voice**; 2) **Reach an audience where they are**; and 3) **Stay focused on basic needs**.

AN IMPORTANT VOICE

Have you ever been in a situation when you're sure you've communicated something in a meeting, no one reacts, but later in the same meeting someone else says the exact same thing and everyone nods in agreement? You find yourself wondering, "Am I crazy... didn't I just say that?" I can't think of many things more cutting and frustrating. It seems to happen quite frequently with public Boards of Directors. It usually looks like this: someone on the senior team expresses a point-of-view or suggests a new strategy. The Board doesn't seem to absorb the message or even respond. When it is restated by the CEO, everyone gets excited. However frustrating this is, none of us should take it personally. Most people, you and I included, don't listen as closely to key communications unless they're coming from our boss or someone we think is important. And who we consider important varies from person to person—and by circumstance to circumstance.

Many times this concept is ignored. Often, the critical duty of providing key communications once a project is in flight is delegated to project managers and corporate trainers. To me, communications can be a powerful, change-activating condition, but only when done well and delivered by the appropriate persons. As such, it requires thoughtfully targeting the senders of messages as much as the receivers. On some occasions, project managers and corporate trainers have the trusted street credibility to provide the reinforcing voice of change; but on other occasions, it must be driven from a position of authority.

My business and life partner, Kristine, tells a story epitomizing this point, which happened to her eight months after she graduated from college. She was a software instructor and had a banking client who just acquired a regional bank. For three weeks, she traveled to the acquired bank's headquarters and delivered software training. Each four-hour training session included a scripted message about technology changes team members were expected to adopt.

As she kicked off her first session, it was clear she was dealing with a hostile group—like, if they had access to tomatoes and rocks they'd throw them kind of hostile. There she was, some strange face delivering a message that their daily work lives would have to change, and soon. As nasty comments and difficult questions were thrown her way, she tried to remain cool and calm, but deep inside she was panicking.

Her scripted messaging didn't give her any information about why these changes were being made. She was clueless about what steps had been taken to facilitate the acquisition and had no idea what other changes these folks were trying to understand and manage. Kristine was asked a lot of questions she couldn't answer. These people were caught off guard and responding from a place of fear and frustration, and she was the messenger. Reflecting on the story, she shared, "I was their ugly face of change!"

In my experience, this story is all too common. Whether it's a consultant on the forefront of a big change, a project manager who is sharing the expectations of executives, or a trainer who is speaking on behalf of the corporation, this kind of proxy message delivery rarely works; the senders are put in a frustrating situation and the receivers completely miss the intended message. Many change initiatives are downstream from larger organizational changes with broader implications. Therefore, it's important the executives who are responsible for the overall vision lay the foundation with messages focused on explaining the WHY. Relying solely on trainers to teach the skills needed for a new process/technology (for example) and provide overall organizational clarity about broader topics is a tall order. It just sets them up for tomatoes in the face.

I'll say—as a former CIO—the same could be said for my own messaging. Clearly, I had a position of authority just like my C-level teammates. However, when I tried to be the sole messenger for large organizational changes that a peer was ultimately accountable for, it didn't work. As an example, if my team was implementing a replacement HR technology product that supported a new performance management process, it wasn't effective for me to be the voice of both changes. Impacted stakeholders may have perceived me as important when it came to talking about the technology itself and why one product was better than another. However, if I tried to communicate the WHY behind the new performance management process without the support of my CEO or executive in charge of HR, the message would get lost in translation. Most people would wonder why IT was pushing a new performance management process and stop listening.

It may be counterintuitive to leaders, but there are many situations when an executive voice isn't considered important by impacted stakeholders. Rather, project leaders and grassroots influencers should become the lead senders for certain messages. As an example, executives should provide the WHY but when people have questions about HOW things are going to get done and in what order, leveraging project managers is best. Furthermore, when people have "word on the street" questions about whether the new change is worth it, they want to hear from trusted peers (whom I keep referring to as grassroots influencers).

I once worked with an executive who had great instincts about whose voice was important to various stakeholders. For instance, when we had town hall meetings and someone asked, "Please explain again why we went down this path to change," he would confidently provide more context about the decision. However, if someone else asked, "Well how are things going with the project," he'd ask a credible, grassroots influencer who was testing the change to provide an update—even prompting for the unfiltered good, bad and ugly. Finally, if someone in the audience asked for details about how the initiative would be implemented, he'd call on the project manager and corporate training team to explain the HOW, WHEN and WHAT.

Important messages deserve important voices—and context determines who we think is important and at what times. I know a lot of people think I'm crazy when I say this, but I really believe attentiveness to communications makes conscious and unconscious impressions on people. I've been in situations where PowerPoint decks were developed and rehearsed by executives in hopes of making them seem prepared and thoughtful. Instead, they came across disingenuous and clueless because they didn't honor the need for relevant, important voices to deliver key parts of the message.

REACH THEM WHERE THEY ARE

Let's regress for a minute. Think back to your teenage years. Yes, it was a funny time, wasn't it? What was your primary means of communication? For me, it was the telephone. And I have to admit, I loved talking on the telephone. I could do it for hours, and often, I would get in trouble for it. Now here's the next question. What's your primary means of communication today? Is it the same as in your teenage years? I bet it's not. For me, it sure isn't. Today, I can't stand talking on the phone.

How about the early days of your career? Did you rely on the phone, email, or perhaps instant messaging? Do you rely on those channels today? How about social tools, texting, or even Snapchatting?

As we all know, communication channels are changing and growing rapidly, every day. Sometimes we completely replace one channel with another. And sometimes, another channel is just an additive to what we're already using. Not only are there multiple channels to consider, we tend to communicate differently in each of those channels. As an example, texting is usually limited to a sentence or two, or maybe even just an emoticon. E-mail is usually a little more detailed or lengthy. Finally, social channels are known to have open threads that go on forever. (I just received a notification the other day, alerting me that someone commented on something I posted on Facebook three years ago!)

To activate people for change, I think it's critical to reach stakeholders where they are and ensure the messaging is customized appropriately for each channel and audience. As an example, the majority of the workforce at Red Robin were millennials. At that time, the data showed millennials were primarily using mobile and social networking—that's where they were. Therefore, our communications strategy had to include social networking and social learning channels with mobile solutions for important messages about change to be absorbed by that demographic. We also learned that while assistant managers were more inclined to use social, general managers still preferred email.

What's key about the Red Robin example is this: different audiences use different channels, and therefore the message was customized for each respective audience. As an example, our President would record video field reports, which he distributed on our social network. There was a large population of assistant managers and restaurant learning coaches using that tool. However, he would still provide messaging in memo form delivered via email to reach general managers.

While the advice about "important messages need important voices" focused on the sender, "reach them where they are" hones in on the relevant channel(s) to reach the receiver. Now, combine that guidance with the right messages and the condition of communications starts activating people for change. But what are the rules of the road for building the right message? It turns out, it's pretty basic.

FOCUS ON BASIC NEEDS

Any interest in trying a social experiment? If so, pick up some donuts on the way to work tomorrow, put them in the break room, and send a message to a group of people announcing, "Free donuts in the break room. Enjoy!"

Most of us have either done this or have been on the receiving end of such a message. If you haven't, try it. There's a pretty predictable outcome—if people don't get to the break room in ten minutes or less, the only thing they'll be doing with the donut is thinking about it. (A funny aside is that a teammate at work did this with those awful, orange marshmallow circus peanuts. I couldn't believe it, but they were gone in no time flat. It just goes to show people will eat anything!)

You don't need me to tell you that pushing large-scale change isn't quite the same—change ain't a box of donuts. Can you imagine if it were? Change leadership would be as simple as, "Brand new HR system in the break room. Enjoy!"

We can learn something from that box of yummy, warm, glazed donuts though. Why does that kind of messaging work with food but not change? Well, food meets a basic need. We don't need reminder messages to entice us when we're hungry. In order for communications to be effective, the message itself has to meet a basic need—the basic need to create awareness and build knowledge.

Recall in the last chapter we explored followership and graduating stakeholders from awareness to understanding to preference. In my opinion, communications should be used to provide awareness, and that's it. I don't believe memos, town hall meetings, and/or PowerPoint decks will ever build the skills and understanding people need to be successful. I also don't believe the words we use or promises we make will ever prompt full-blown preference for a disruptive change. So, why use fancy, persuasive messaging that may cause confusion rather than provide clarity? That approach just comes across as a sales pitch. Rather, share the bare essentials and ensure your stakeholders are adequately aware of what they need to know—for instance, an action-oriented WHAT supported by an enlisting WHY. But communication has to stop there. Other conditions, which we will soon explore, are better suited to build understanding and preference.

Change leaders have to be realistic about what communications can and cannot accomplish. Words alone cannot convince people to get on board with some new Thing. Words alone can, however, raise awareness.

"We're going to focus more on growing and developing our people by implementing a new talent management system," is much more effective than, "This company is the greatest place to work because we provide the best growth and development opportunities on the planet!"

AND ANOTHER THING...

Probably in the category of random advice but too important not to mention: corporate communications tend to be neutered from time to time and therefore lose their effectiveness. In our coaching and consultancy work, Kristine and I jokingly refer to "Dr. Seuss language" when we read these types of memos and legal documents or hear confusing speeches. The related messages sound like they are being communicated in riddles and rhymes! Dr. Seuss language usually takes one of two forms.

First, leaders are often convinced they must communicate something to their teams during a tumultuous period of change (such as organizational restructurings or projects gone bad). However, they are then intentionally ambiguous to avoid hurting anyone's feelings or to disguise realities (like impending layoffs) which might prematurely scare people away. Have you ever been on the receiving end of a memo that states, "The executive leadership team is considering potential options for reorganizing the company to gain efficiencies in our operations?" Or how about, "Our new technology implementation is not meeting our current objectives, and as such, the team is exploring various alternatives?" This type of messaging just isn't helpful. The whole point of communications is to raise awareness. Neither of the examples above do that. Instead, they are teasers that create confusion as team members mince words to find true meaning.

This same point holds true for the second reason Dr. Seuss language occurs in corporate communications—compliance. In an increasingly litigious society and regulated business world (especially for public companies), leaders are fearful communications will later be used to justify a complaint or lawsuit. As a result, written and verbal communications are constructed in a measured way with legalese and disclaimers. The result is once again confusion; instead of building knowledge with impacted stakeholders, everyone's left scratching their heads wondering what the communications actually meant.

More and more, we hear about the importance of transparency. However, what's even more impactful than transparency is clarity. Vomiting a few carefully crafted, politically correct messages might provide transparency, but it does nothing for providing clarity. And when communications don't provide clarity, the related message is either ignored or triggers a slew of "water cooler" conversations that only build resistance for change later down the road.

In summary, the key is to deliver authentic messaging with humanness and clarity. If you don't, team members have another reason to mistrust (or disconnect from) leaders. Ineffective communications creates noise, and people (consciously or unconsciously) will filter that noise and disengage. And disengagement definitely doesn't help with adoption!

ACTIVATING PEOPLE FOR CHANGE

LEARNING

The top reasons team members leave organizations include not being developed; the top reasons leaders aren't winning with change include their team members not having requisite skills to be successful. It's a win-win when leaders utilize learning as a centerpiece in their change activation strategy—performance is improved and retention goes up.

With communications, impacted stakeholders gain awareness of a new change, but the benefits usually stop there. Generally, people need skill-building to achieve true understanding about something new, and the condition of learning does just that. But don't be fooled: learning is more than memorization activities. Rather, learning provides an opportunity to apply and practice new skills, and is most impactful when it includes collaborative sharing.

For some organizations, learning is an organizational mindset and cultural tenet that encourages team members to continually seek knowledge, explore, and experiment with an open mind. This leadership approach provides a safety net by reinforcing that failing is okay and part of the growing process.

CHAPTER 9

A GUN TO THE HEAD
(LEARNING)

"Tell me and I forget.

Teach me and I remember.

Involve me and I learn."

—Benjamin Franklin

IGNITING A LOVE OF LEARNING

When I was a kid, I got really excited when my father thought I was old enough to mow our lawn. I know that may sound weird, but there was something "coming of age" about being able to press my 120-pound body up against the lawn mower handle—and getting the opportunity to completely destroy tall grass! (Maybe it's a boy thing?) My dad was really thrifty so we used an old Briggs & Stratton mower that had been around for ages. This thing was full of mechanical problems.

In particular, the mower was always hard to start. One Saturday afternoon when I couldn't get it to fire up, my dad wanted to train me on how to troubleshoot the issue. I was eager to learn how to manage this beast. He quickly talked me through a checklist of items to consider, which included a kludgy method of engaging the spark plug since the connector was hit or miss; I was instructed to use a screwdriver as a proxy for the faulty wire to get a start. My dad sure made it sound easy. He had me off and mowing in no time flat.

A few weeks later on a hot, summer day in Florida, I couldn't get the mower to start. It was time to apply what my dad taught me. Running through his checklist was a memorization activity, which included recalling things to evaluate as well as the safety measures I needed to use in the process. I grabbed a screwdriver, and in a determined manner, put the metal up against the spark plug. I however missed a critical step. My hand wasn't on the insulated handle of the screwdriver like my dad warned when he explained the technique. I was gripping the metal inches from the contact point. As you can imagine, I got the shock of my life!

After being thrown backwards a few feet, it was clear that talk alone wasn't going to get me very far in life. And after many years and similar experiences in my corporate career, I think the same can be said about matters related to change.

Most of us have heard the saying, "talk is cheap." And most of us know that rework, turnover, and physical accidents aren't. But that's exactly what results when leaders only use written and verbal communications to activate change. You see, even where there's a will, there isn't always a way when you lack true understanding. Despite my best intentions to start the lawn mower on that hot, humid day, I simply lacked the skills I needed to get the job done.

SHIFTING OUR MINDSET

I've always been intrigued with the military and professional sports. One profession deals with life and death and wields powerful weapons; the other involves winning and losing a game and leverages recreational equipment. Despite their obvious differences, both require an ironman will and a deep level of understanding in order to succeed. In the corporate world, we would label that kind of commitment as nothing less than true engagement.

Imagine for a moment a professional football coach. He calls his team into the locker room, delivers a well-written speech and outlines the game plan for an upcoming match-up. During his speech, he informs the players that their typical strategy of running the ball won't work. Instead, they'll be passing. This is a big change for a rough and tumble team who is accustomed to a slower moving, smash mouth approach. At the end of his speech, he dismisses the players and tells them he'll see them on Sunday.

Now imagine a military leader. He brings together a trusted group of lieutenants to announce a big change. While they've been in a demilitarized mode for quite some time, he's enlisting them to engage in battle. He delivers a well-written speech that outlines his strategy and includes words of motivation. He ensures everyone knows their assignments and tells them he hopes to see them on Sunday.

I'm sure you know by now that it doesn't work that way in professional sports, and it surely doesn't work that way in the military. Rather, both athletes and soldiers undergo intense learning that involves active simulations, integrated training (physical fitness and fundamentals), safe zones to fail, relentless practice, and real-time peer feedback. While the military and professional sports teams may use the word, "training" to describe preparation and practice, I think their approach is more about learning. It's the type of experience that's engaging; it's motivating; it builds followership and loyalty. Wouldn't it be amazing if corporate teams did the same when they were rolling out a big change? Talk about encouraging an iron will with your team members!

Training, in the corporate sense, often involves memorization activities and looks like, "Follow these steps to achieve this outcome." (For example, my lawn mower experience and many software self-help systems.) The problem is, this method is the lowest level of learning and just doesn't provide enough practice for people to apply and master new skills. Yet, we as leaders often expect uncompromised adherence to standards with consistent, "pie in the sky" results. Therefore, our teams feel anxious, unfulfilled and their retention is low. A true learning mindset, however, encourages and nurtures the application of new concepts and builds proficiency and confidence. When this shift becomes reality, it maximizes a team member's engagement level, who will then become more invested in the future.

So, what can leaders learn from the military, professional sports and my failed lawn mowing days? What should you consider, and how can you make the shift from a culture of memorization to learning?

It starts with acknowledging that speeches, memos, PowerPoint decks and self-help user guides can only go so far. At some point, team members need to understand their role in change and be given the opportunity to build the skills they need to be successful; this only happens with learning. And, as with communications, it's a requirement that executives, project leaders and grassroots influencers each do their part. What I've experienced across many change initiatives is there are certain elements needed to promote the condition of learning. It may not be what leaders expect, but **Failing, Mastery** and **Sharing** can provide the kind of experiential learning that activates people for change.

FAILING IS LEARNING

As I started writing this book, I had many conversations with former colleagues and folks in my personal network about the words "fail" and "failure." These conversations, along with my own life lessons, caused me to be very measured when using either term. From a leadership perspective, I strongly believe failure is not the opposite of success. Rather, I believe failure is a step in the process of achieving success.

Organizations and executive leaders who nurture and embrace failure are a step ahead in the world of change leadership. When corporate cultures encourage seeking knowledge, exploration, and experimentation, you will readily observe people activated for change. Think about it—if you aren't afraid of making a mistake, you will be more likely to try something new. Conversely, if a heavy-

FAILURE

Failure is not the opposite of success. Rather, failure is a step in the process of achieving success.

handed micromanager critically judges even the smallest of errors, it would push you into a fight or flight mode.

You may have heard the expression, "fail fast!" It's used by teams and leaders who challenge the status quo and implement disruptive innovation. I suggest we make a small change to the expression so it's better aligned with what I think is its true intention, "learn fast!" To support a "learn fast" approach, it makes the most sense to deliver and manage change in small doses. When smaller, incremental wins are achieved, the momentum is infectious and encourages people to keep trying. Even more importantly, smaller doses of change make mistakes and failure less catastrophic to a total organization. I once heard an IT leader describe this approach as, "Think big; start small; iterate fast!" I can't think of a better way to summarize a "learn fast" philosophy.

As you've probably noticed, I've included a few warnings in this book. This is a subject that deserves one such warning, and here it is. Anyone trying to build a "fail fast" or "learn fast" culture has to stay true to their word. Environments that encourage failure in words but punish it in actions will paralyze people's activation for change. Guaranteed. I know this advice seems obvious, but it happens all the time. Some examples of conscious or unconscious punishment in the work world include an over-reliance of vanity metrics such as on-time, on-budget, and in-scope during experimentation and prototyping; providing negative feedback in a performance review regarding sub-optimal innovation cycles and; withholding future investments in research and development because of past "failures."

Looking back now to that fateful folly with my dad's mower, I can see the importance of failure in my own learning. I never practiced or applied the checklist he created under his supervision, and I overly relied on my memorization skills to help me in a "live" troubleshooting moment. Since an effective learning opportunity was missed, it took an unfortunately shocking moment to permanently etch in my brain how important safety procedures are when handling small or large equipment. And I can assure you, the same is true for team members in an organization. Failing is truly learning. So rather than it happen accidentally, plan for and accept it!

MASTERY IS LEARNING

In his groundbreaking book, *Drive: The Surprising Truth About What Motivates Us,* Daniel Pink identifies a few things that are important in motivating team members— and contrary to the intuition of most, it isn't variable rewards and bonuses. As an example, Pink talks about the importance of mastery, which he simply and elegantly defines as, "The urge to get better at stuff." To the extent project leaders provide people opportunities to get better at stuff, those same people will become more engaged and motivated. And when those learning opportunities come from a change, team members will undoubtedly show more interest.

This takes me back to the new learning platform we developed at Red Robin, which was reviewed in Chapter

5, *The Easy Button (Design).* If you recall: the charter for this project was to address the challenges of new-hire onboarding, which was fueled by an alarming turnover rate. In addition, we wanted to provide our team members a more relevant and impactful way to build their skills.

We were handing team members a mammoth training manual and asking them to memorize our standard operating procedures, and as a result, new hires were struggling to retain key information and exhibit desired behaviors. This had a negative effect on our guests and team members. Clearly, it was time for change.

During the project, we uncovered that our team members didn't feel like they were getting enough practice time developing new skills needed to succeed at their job. But in the case of Red Robin, practice meant throwing away food and beverage or trying something new with live guests in the restaurant—practice was costly and risky. However, our team members were consistently expressing "the urge to get better at stuff." Therefore, we knew we had to adjust our views on practice.

You already know the solution was an iPad-based platform filled with interactive games and simulations, demonstration videos, and a social network. I'll cover the demonstration videos and social network later, but I want to focus on the interactive games and simulations for a minute. Those modules provided the right practice ground for our team members to develop their skills and get better at stuff, without wasting food or disappointing a guest. Instead, they enjoyed games designed to simulate our kitchen, bar, and guests all while accumulating points on a leaderboard (thus proving their mastery).

Because of our industry and workforce demographic, this solution was appropriate for encouraging skill building. If games and simulations aren't appropriate in your environment, then find solutions that are. Be sure to give your team the time and tools they need to get better at stuff. That is what's important. I should also say, we didn't purely rely on games and simulations to build mastery. Team members were given the opportunity to shadow their teammates and reinforce their knowledge in a live environment.

Within months of the new learning platform being in place, we received amazing reviews from restaurant managers about the improved engagement and performance of team members. And wouldn't you know it, retention started to increase, too.

SHARING IS LEARNING

Another key element of learning is sharing. Team members, millennials in particular, like to share new ideas and their own mastery with other team members. In addition, they like the opportunity to learn from others who have walked a mile in their shoes. This means peer-to-peer, grassroots influence can go a long way with evangelizing change and promoting organizational learning.

Earlier, I promised to cover the video and social network components of the Red Robin iPad learning solution. Our team members were encouraged to use the video capability of the iPad to film themselves demonstrating new or better methods for existing standards. Those videos could be uploaded to an integrated social network, allowing our corporate teams to review each submission. If these methods were found to add value, the content would be published for community consumption and the sharing team member would be the "star of the show" with his or her peers.

The social network wasn't just a place for team members to upload videos. It was also a resource for discussing and sharing. As an example, if a brand standard required further clarification, team members could interact with each other and our Learning and Development team to learn more details. Those discussions provided real-time feedback about concepts that may not be resonating with the team members and might require further exploration or skill building. Again, people aren't always forthcoming when they don't understand something so this is an awesome method for receiving clues about potential disconnects.

While video demonstrations and social networks provide platforms for sharing, they certainly don't replace the need for human interaction and face-to-face, peer feedback. Instead, they simply provide a way to reach people at scale, as well as provide a channel of preference for some team members. But just like communications, sharing has to reach people where they are. There has to be authenticity and interaction to nurture connection.

This makes me think about a meet-up that occurs in my neighborhood. I've driven by it several times on a Saturday morning when taking my kids to their Tae-Kwon-Do studio. The owners of restored muscle cars from the 50's and 60's pop their hoods up and proudly share the engine and detail work of their prized possession. Now mind you, I've never actually participated in the festivities, but I picture the kind of conversations that occur. "How did you do that? Where did you find that part? How fast can she go?" It's not hard to imagine because I've gone to church, done group fitness, and belong to industry organizations—all serving a similar purpose. People like to learn from others and share their own knowledge, as well. Encouraging a culture of peer coaching, modeling and support goes a long way toward building the acceptance and adoption of change.

A SIMPLE LITMUS TEST

After reviewing the elements needed to promote the condition of learning and skill building, I want to relay an important caveat that a well-respected Learning and Development leader once shared with me. In her words, "If a team member had a gun held to his head and would know how to do what we're asking him to do, then learning strategies aren't the answer!" Let me clarify.

I've seen many leaders jump right to "training" as an answer to non-compliance for large-scale change initiatives. That is, when mediocre results are being achieved and team members don't seem fully engaged in change, leaders assume the right learning methods weren't used. However, if it can be determined that team members know exactly what's expected of them, then awareness (aided by communications) and understanding (aided by learning) aren't the issues; preference is.

And when preference is the issue, it's time to leverage conditions that influence people's motivation to care. In my opinion, nothing does that more effectively than stakeholder engagement... so, let's move on!

ACTIVATING PEOPLE FOR CHANGE

STAKEHOLDER ENGAGEMENT

With so much emphasis on communications and teaching, it's easy to forget the need for listening. However, it is the leaders who encourage feedback and provide demonstrable action as a result that win the hearts of team members. And when this happens, people are more willing to accept something new.

During the deployment of large-scale change, project and executive leaders need to constantly check the pulse of impacted stakeholders. How? One-to-one conversations, focus groups, town hall meetings, human-centered design sessions and social networks all serve as important inputs to an organization's health. The more channels, the better. However, take warning: leaders ought not ask for feedback if they don't plan on doing anything with it.

Change resistance usually occurs when people

feel like they are on a dead-end street and no one is listening to or addressing their concerns. But when top of mind matters for team members become top of mind matters for leaders, it creates an environment of safety and trust. Safety and trust promotes hope and optimism—which drives preference. And preference, of course, leads to true change and transformation!

CHAPTER 10

DUMBO COMES TO MIND
(STAKEHOLDER ENGAGEMENT)

"The greatest compliment that was ever paid me was when one asked me what I thought, and attended to my answer."

–Henry David Thoreau

"YOU'RE NOT COMMUNICATING!"

During my Red Robin years, I always looked forward to our Quarterly Ops meetings. Every three months, we met with our best operators around the country, always in a different location. We had two goals for these meetings. First, we wanted to reward and recognize a small group of our top restaurant managers and regional directors. Second, we wanted to talk about what was and was not working in the business so we could continually improve our operations. During these meetings, I learned some important lessons about change leadership...

I think the most impactful lesson came from the first Ops meeting I attended, which was in Key Largo, Florida. Unbeknown to me, attendees were following a fairly predictable agenda with business meetings on day one, a celebration outing on day two and a wonderfully orchestrated awards dinner to cap off the activities. As was the tradition, prior to dismissing the group for their celebration outing, there was an important hour-long meeting in the morning. During this session, we sat in a big circle, and in a "nameless, rankless" manner, participants had the opportunity to provide direct feedback about their current pain points. As the new guy, I couldn't have attended a better session since I was still assembling my list of top priorities; I was eager to hear what the group had to say.

Managers and directors alike took turns offering up their challenges. One particular theme was sticking out like a sore thumb—communications. While each person phrased it a little differently, most of the time it sounded like, "Communications is lacking," or "Our leaders need to communicate more." As I sat back and observed the outpouring of tough love, I was struck by how seriously my executive peers were taking this feedback. It was obvious the subject was going to receive an action plan once we returned to headquarters.

The effort back home was impressive. Many of the organization's top cross-functional leaders mobilized to focus on the theme of field communications. In the end, we decided the most direct path to solving the problem was to create a well-organized "Weekly Mailer," a solution that packaged all organizational memos together and delivered them in a single, weekly distribution. Included in the approach was the templatizing of "Action Required" versus "Information Only" memos. It was decided the corporate operations team would own the mailer and provide quality control on the content to ensure consistency, clear language, and a common voice. Seems like an appropriate response to the feedback, doesn't it?

Soon after our return from the offsite, the newly minted Weekly Mailer was implemented. I have to say, I was really impressed with the whole process—ranging from the constructive manner in which operators communicated a pain point all the way to the immediate attention executive leaders gave to an action plan. As a new team member, I was positively impacted by this demonstration of collaboration and open leadership, and just downright proud to be part of the team. I could hardly wait to attend the next Quarterly Ops meeting and hear how the solution was making a difference.

Our next gathering was in Bend, Oregon. Again, the meeting followed the typical agenda and on the morning of our planned celebration outing, everyone sat in a circle to discuss what was and was not working. It didn't take long for the group to start rallying around the theme of communications. I thought, "Here we go! Just bask in the praise they're getting ready to shower us with." However, to my surprise, instead of making the list of things working well, communications once again topped the list of things not working well. What?!? How could this be? The Weekly Mailer process seemed so much more organized and cohesive than the way we previously managed things. Yet attendees were still saying, "You aren't communicating." Despite our best efforts, the executives knew that action-planning communications was once again on our to-do list.

If I cut to the chase, this cycle repeated itself several times… for close to two years! The good news is, in every instance it resulted in an evolved method for communicating to the field. The bad news is, we just couldn't crack the code on a topic that was clearly causing pain for our operators.

A few years after that initial meeting in Key Largo, a new truth struck me. I wish I could point to the source of revelation. It may have been a statement an operator made in a group meeting, or it may have come from a side conversation with a peer. Obviously, the story would be more epic if I could remember what seeded such an important discovery—one that would change how I thought about communications going forward. You see, I realized when people said we weren't communicating, what they really meant was… we weren't LISTENING!

TUNE IN YOUR LISTENING EARS

As a kid, I frequently got in trouble for my big mouth. Teachers and parents constantly told me, "Chris, you need to tune in your listening ears." One teacher even suggested, "Pretend you're Dumbo and that your ears are bigger than your whole body!" As a child, I didn't necessarily understand or appreciate the importance of that recommendation. However, those words came to mind years later when I had my aha moment about listening versus communicating.

I know now that listening is the single most important tactic used to activate people for change—and is the key to stakeholder engagement. Just like when I was a kid, most of my professional mistakes came at times when I was

Tuning in our listening ears can
help us win the hearts of our team
members and inspire them to care.

doing more talking than listening, or listening haphazardly. My biggest victories, however, came at times when I was wearing my "Dumbo ears."

Tuning in our listening ears can help us win the hearts of our team members and inspire them to care. And when this happens, it invites our stakeholders to be part of the change rather than just receivers of it. That type of engagement makes everyone stronger and drives exponential success.

As an example, imagine the power of saying, "We've received feedback from all of you that you would like more career development, and we agree that this is something we should focus on. As such, we will be moving forward on a project to implement Talent Management software." In a single statement, you've aligned people to the WHY, which was sourced directly from them while listening to their feedback. Furthermore, you've enlisted them to take action on their own needs while providing knowledge about a new tool you're hoping they'll adopt. In essence, you've raised awareness and started to capture their hearts (preference) all in one simple sentence!

But beware—there are a couple of things leaders need to consider before they start building and advertising a listening campaign. First, when leaders only pretend to listen, their messaging will give it away. I know it sounds obvious, but think about it. How many times have you heard a leader talk about an upcoming change after eliciting feedback from their teams and thought, "They have no clue!" Or, "Where did that come from?" When leaders fail to capture the true essence of the feedback provided, the disconnectedness of the idea shines through. And this will block preference time and time again.

Second, only ask for input if you mean it. A respected friend of mine, Hayes Drumwright, the Founder and CEO of PoPin, has brilliantly pointed out, "Most people think the worst thing leaders can do is not ask people for their opinion. But the worst thing leaders can do is ask people for their opinion and then do nothing about it!" Listening does little to win the hearts of our team members if we don't actually take action on the feedback we're receiving. In fact, doing nothing after you listen could downright hurt your reputation and followership.

So, with that said: how do we corporately tune in our listening ears? The chosen methods, of course, depend on an organization's culture and the individual personalities of the executive leaders. But taking into account what we learned in the communications chapter, reaching the intended audience where they are is also an important part of the listening equation. Based on my experiences, I believe the most relevant and effective methods for listening and engaging stakeholders include: **Town Halls and Focus Groups, Human-Centered Design,** and **Social Networking.**

TOWN HALLS AND FOCUS GROUPS

When I think of town hall meetings, I can't help but think about politicians who travel around the country to share their ideas and answer questions from constituents. Now, I know many of us are cynical about the campaign process currently used in America. Nonetheless, there isn't any level of negative sentiment that discounts the power of sharing ideas and getting instant feedback from a community of impacted stakeholders.

When I think of focus groups, I immediately think about funny commercials—the kind that show a small panel of people testing or trying a product together and providing unfiltered reactions. Just like with politicians, there are cynical people who don't trust marketers. But again, you can't dismiss the value of getting feedback from a group of potential customers.

So, while some may think politicians and marketers are filthy and untrustworthy salespeople, change leaders can learn a thing or two from them. The fact is that town halls and focus groups can be applied in a corporate setting to beautifully achieve stakeholder engagement. Yet, I'm always surprised to hear that so few organizations use them to activate change. I've heard a variety of excuses for not doing them, ranging from scalability to confidentiality to budget constraints. Honestly, I shake my head at these reasons and wonder why organizations would even attempt to drive change without some form of town hall meeting or focus group. Getting a group of impacted stakeholders together in person to share ideas, answer their questions and receive feedback is essential to building a working atmosphere of trust and confidence.

But does this stakeholder engagement method require anything special or unique to be effective? Yes—values. Let me explain. When I was at Red Robin, the culture honored team members and reinforced seeking knowledge as one of the company's core values. Therefore, the high-touch manner in which the Quarterly Ops meeting (a focus group) was structured was an excellent way to get honest, face-to-face input from key influencers and restaurant leaders. People felt safe because they knew leaders really wanted to hear their feedback, even if it was full of conflict. Unfortunately, this isn't the case for every culture. For example, if you're a command-and-control, top-down executive leader or a project leader who is working with an executive who is, I wholeheartedly believe town halls and focus groups aren't the method for you. Because if executive leaders use body language and/or words that say people's feedback doesn't really matter, the whole tactic will backfire.

I can recall being in a town hall meeting where a top-down CEO unveiled a new plan he was working on with the Board. He invited the audience to ask questions and provide feedback. Unfortunately, as more and more questions were asked, he became progressively agitated. He even went as far in future town hall meetings to reference that situation and say, "Now when we get to the Q&A section of my talk, we aren't going to have a repeat of the town hall where we discussed the _____ initiative." You can imagine what that did for stakeholder engagement and preference.

HUMAN-CENTERED DESIGN

A second suggestion for promoting stakeholder engagement, which was detailed in Chapter 5: *The Easy Button (Design)*, is to leverage human-centered design.

Key points about how this method works to support the condition of Design can be found there. As it relates to stakeholder engagement, a critical ingredient is that stakeholders be involved prior to selecting or designing a solution. Said another way, people often believe leaders are not actually interested in their feedback (or that they just aren't listening) when they are asked to get involved only *after* a decision has been made.

As an example, I once talked to a realtor who worked for one of the largest brokers in the country. She noted the company asked her for feedback on a new contract management system, *after* it was already decided the old system was going to be replaced. It was nice that her leadership team wanted her to review the new technology, but she was quick to point out: had they talked to the realtors to begin with, the leadership team would have found that the realtors' pain points actually had nothing to do with the old contract management system. In fact, she said the word on the street was most realtors really liked the old system. Oops.

SOCIAL NETWORKING

A final way to corporately listen, which I strongly favor, is the use of social networking tools. For the first time, the millennial generation is the largest cohort in the U.S. workforce, and the data shows that they're massive users of social networking. It's almost as if they came out of the womb providing thoughts and input through web interfaces and apps. So, leveraging social tools is absolutely how you can reach this demographic where they are!

There are many great options in the marketplace, but perhaps the biggest breakthrough concept that I've used is a mobile engagement app called PoPin. (And I'm not just saying that because I'm friends with Hayes. I'd tell him, and you, if I thought his offering stunk!) With this tool, executive or project leaders can run "sessions" with impacted stakeholders to ask open-ended questions such as, "What is the greatest pain point preventing you from being successful at work?" Unlike surveys, which give predetermined answers, impacted stakeholders can provide unconstrained responses, and then others can vote each submission up (love it) or down (hate it). Whether you use PoPin or not, the key idea is this: don't seed an audience with preconceived notions about their pain points or preferred solutions. When you do, opportunities are often missed.

While asking open ended questions lets you get closer to reality more quickly, it's sometimes harder to curate the responses and understand themes at scale. I get it. This is one reason many organizations stick with boring surveys. But using a social networking tool that has a voting feature (likes/dislikes) helps solve that challenge by creating a common voice around a particular matter. This method is especially effective during the testing or implementation of a change. As an example, after an initial pilot release of new software, you could ask team members, "Now that you've worked with the new system, what would you change before it is released to anyone else?" Talk about crowd solving and stakeholder engagement at its finest!

Of course, reaching out via social networking also enables listening at scale. So, if you're using scalability as an excuse for not using town hall meetings or focus groups, this is the method for you. With social tools, a leader's listening campaign can include a large group of people in various demographic regions—without having to deal with scheduling hassles.

In summary, a leader's willingness and capability to listen reinforces that progress is being made and stakeholders shouldn't panic if something appears to be off track. Conversely, failure to listen often causes grassroots influencers to stop working and dig in on issues, which impacts a team's ability to move forward. This response often occurs when they realize they only have one shot to get it right (in organizations that don't leverage feedback). So, they go on strike, so to speak—and often during critical activities like testing and implementation. When this happens, disenchantment spreads like cancer to other team members. And obviously, that's not good for anybody.

TAKE IT, TWEAK IT, SHARE IT

I believe the more listening tools leveraged, the better. A large and diverse toolbox reinforces a culture of seeking knowledge and builds confidence that if things don't go as planned, leaders will quickly pivot. After all, there's nothing more demoralizing than being in an environment that insists on pushing forward with dead-end processes or technologies. You know, the ones that everyone knows are losers but no one has the courage to challenge?

Some leaders believe this kind of thinking is "soft and squishy." However, I'd like to point out that very real and tangible benefits exist for companies as they innovate and continuously improve their operations. And that outcome is only possible when there's a strong connection between the grassroots influencers and top leaders. And most of the time, team members closest to the action (and the customers) know a lot more about pain points and opportunities than their leaders. Capturing those ideas can be invaluable... so why not ask them?

Let me share an example that highlights the power of listening to drive an outcome of innovation and continuous improvement. This story ties into what I've already shared about deploying iPads system-wide at Red Robin. As we explored the idea, we realized how imperative it was to solve many complex operational issues related to procuring, securing, and updating the devices across all our restaurants. Since the technology was so new, the real difficulty wasn't necessarily *solving* the issues—it was understanding the kind of operational challenges that might arise once we started our deployment. We didn't know what we didn't know. So, asking for help seemed like a good place to start.

We decided to engage stakeholders on a volunteer basis by issuing an innovation challenge on Yammer, the company's social network. The challenge enticed restaurant managers to volunteer their stores to experiment with the iPads. All they had to do was provide a few sentences about why their restaurant should be selected and agree there would be no formal support channels to solve their initial problems. Instead, they would have to take it, tweak it and share it. That is, once they got the iPads (take it) and started experiencing problems, they would have to discover a solution, adjust their implementation (tweak it), and publish the details of the solution in a public forum on Yammer so others had access to the fix (share it).

Fifty-two restaurants participated in the program and this experiment created an awesome mechanism for collaboration and building a change network of grassroots influencers. In addition, it reassured restaurant managers that these new Things would never take precedence over them as People. Instead, they knew this was an experiment that empowered them to provide feedback and make recommendations for the ultimate solution. They also understood that if the proof-of-concept didn't produce fruitful results, we'd never move forward with a system-wide deployment. This approach nurtured a healthy and rapid innovation process that quickly set Red Robin up to be one of the first national chains to integrate iPads in their day-to-day operations.

THE MAKING OF AN ACCOMPLICE

While making people feel valued and tapping into their invaluable experiences was the principal focus, there were additional outcomes and benefits worth talking about from the iPad example—the kind of things that can transform an organization.

First, corporate listening helped us enroll people in a cause. It didn't mean buy-in was fully there, but it began the necessary process of identifying a change network that transcended org charts and job descriptions; a network that ultimately helped us drive change adoption in the field. You see, while some operators were excited about the notion of iPads in their restaurants, others thought the devices would be too hard to secure and manage and didn't want the hassle.

Second, it reinforced that done isn't done if it isn't right. A lot of resistance to change comes from people who fear incomplete, irrelevant, or defective solutions. They're concerned the new Thing will pollute their work quality or make life harder. This was certainly the case with the iPads—while managers could visualize using them at home, there were some that were worried that they'd never stand up to the wear and tear that can happen in a busy restaurant. Engaging team members in dialog along the way and putting meaningful action and remedies into place will reinforce if things aren't going as planned, they will be corrected. This mindset results in people being much more willing to adopt a new change. Even better, as Hayes Drumwright has noted, "They're willing to be an accomplice in the process!" Talk about preference.

ACTIVATING PEOPLE FOR CHANGE

SUPPORT

o

Credibility = Track Record + Empathy. There's no better way to build track record or demonstrate empathy than by meeting people's very basic need to be supported. Team members will only have preference and willingly adopt a new change, if they received solid support during the last big change.

However, for most organizations, support is an afterthought. As a result, it's become a societal norm for people to receive mediocre help, at best, when something doesn't go as planned. As an example, have you ever been trapped in an automated telephone system that eventually routes you to another time zone with someone who is in no position to help? How do you feel after that experience? Have you ever discontinued a contract or stopped using a product as a result?

To activate people for change, high-touch support is critical—especially during the early stages of something new. And let's be real. High-touch support requires investment... but we also know that lack of adoption is costly. Many business cases for large-scale technology change contemplate benefits in perpetuity. However, planning for support investments in perpetuity is typically not considered. Leaders must assume systems will require significant enhancements over time as business conditions and assumptions change. If they don't, they risk losing trust with people. And when trust is lost, future transformation becomes exponentially harder.

CHAPTER 11

LIFETIME WARRANTY (SUPPORT)

"Technology... is a queer thing. It brings you great gifts with one hand, and it stabs you in the back with the other."

—Carrie Snow

OPENING DOORS

A number of years ago, my family and I lived in a 1921 bungalow that had a detached garage. Soon after we moved in, the garage door stopped working. We weren't even settled, and I was already questioning whether or not this new Thing we purchased was a turd. Typically, my method of operation is to call in an expert when something is broken at home. There are many things I'm proud of, but my ability to fix things around the house isn't at the top of the list. I'm just not mechanically inclined. (Remember the lawnmower incident?) I, however, decided to turn over a new leaf and therefore proclaimed to the Mrs., "I'm going to start being a little more handy around the home—and this is the perfect project to start with!"

My newfound interest took me to YouTube. With very little effort, I was able to find a long list of instructional videos, which seemingly taught everything you need to know about the mechanics of a garage door. Toward the top of the search list was a six-minute, how-to video on troubleshooting common issues. "Perfect!" With a whole lot of optimism, I clicked on the link and watched the video end-to-end. Just to make sure I was covering my bases, I decided to watch it a second time—and if you can believe it, a third. Eighteen minutes later, I was feeling eager to practice what I learned. I practically ran to the garage!

Promptly, I went through my checklist of potential issues, but everything appeared to be in working condition. I decided I might have rushed the troubleshooting process so I went through my list of considerations again, this time more thoroughly. After multiple passes, I was sure everything was operable. "I don't get it," I thought to myself. "I've checked everything the expert said I should check. He said this was a list of common issues. Is it me? Did I miss something? This sure looked a whole lot easier on video."

After 30 minutes of troubleshooting, I gave up; I picked up the phone and called a garage door expert. Someone was at the house in the next few hours to diagnose the issue. Uncharacteristically, I decided to shadow the expert so I could see where I might have gone wrong. We walked into the garage and in less than 10 seconds, he matter-of-factly said, "Your spring is busted," and pointed to the broken component. I stood there with my mouth wide open. How could a six-minute instructional video positioned to help with common issues not even say one word about a key component like a spring? I couldn't help but wonder, "How many garage doors did the creator of that video actually fix in his lifetime?"

From this experience, I developed more empathy than ever for team members who struggle with technology. You see, when something stops (or never starts) working as planned, they usually try to self-diagnose the problem by reviewing a list of frequently asked questions or using a Help function. When doing this, they assume whoever assembled the information knew with great certainty what the common issues really were. Yet, after lost time and productivity and much defeat, the team member is often forced to pick up the phone and call for help. If they're as lucky as I was with the garage door incident, someone shows up or calls back in a timely fashion. When the whole mess concludes, they're happy to be back up and running but can't help but wonder why their issue wasn't included in the help materials to begin with. Just like that, trust is shaken—because the team member assumes the systems engineers aren't even connected to the everyday needs of the end-users.

There's one more parallel between my garage door incident and technology in the work world that increased my empathy level. It turns out that since the house and garage were built so long ago, the spring actually had to be custom made. This reality added cost and time to my home repair project, and of course was not covered by any kind of warranty. Being the novice that I was, I was surprised to learn not all garage doors operate with standard components. The expert told me that I had a unique need, and it wasn't going to be an easy task to fix the issue. Sound familiar? It should. This scenario happens quite frequently in companies when technology products stop working and require detailed and time-consuming customizations to fix.

YOUR LAST EXPERIENCE DEFINES THE NEXT EXPERIENCE

The worst casualty resulting from my garage door experience wasn't that I had to pay someone to fix the problem. It was my newfound reluctance to take on even the simplest of home repair projects. I concluded that if a six-minute, how-to video on common garage door issues didn't cover the basics like the stupid spring, I might eventually step on other landmines in the battlegrounds of home repairs. I was frightened to think about what might have happened if I were troubleshooting an electrical issue. (Again, remember the lawn mower incident?) From that point forward, I became resistant to taking on new "honey do" tasks when things around the house were broken... even when my wife reminded me of my proclamation.

This is the same challenge change leaders have on their hands. For instance, if a change was pushed last year, and it didn't go as planned, team members will be reluctant and might even resist anything slightly resembling that prior experience. Even worse, if the change didn't go as planned and they didn't receive good compensating support, they certainly don't want to hear about anything new. And who can blame them? These negative experiences would certainly block preference, and ultimately adoption, for the best of us.

This reminds me of a story from early in my career, one that reinforces this very point. Only a few years out of college and into my first job, I was put in charge of a big project—and it was time for "Go Live." I was rolling out a new system that I had both designed and developed. While I was part of a very small IT team, the impact of the new software would be felt broadly by all of our team members, spanning across 13 offices around the world. From administrative assistants to middle management to Vice Presidents to Executives: every day, almost every team member would use the software at least once. This was my chance to shine, but day one in production indicated there may be dark skies in the forecast.

The early Monday a.m. ringing of my telephone after the long, weekend deployment was the first sign I might have failed. I picked up the phone, and one of my favorite coworkers was on the other end. Her name was Liz and before my ear even touched the receiver, I heard her cackling, "Prrrrroooooooobbbllllleeem!" After chatting with her for a minute, I hung up and hurried to her desk. During my walk down the hall, I quickly reflected on the six months it took me to port our old system into a newer platform. I started to wonder if all the effort was really worth it—and whether I should be updating my resume!

When I reached Liz, she was fairly aggressive and probably acting as the mouthpiece for the entire company. "No one knows why we upgraded our system. The old one was perfectly fine. The new one takes longer to do a look-up, and I can't do a print-screen." After poking around on her computer for a few minutes, I found the issue, triaged it, and calmly explained to her it wasn't the new software that was slow. Instead, her computer was getting to the end of its shelf life; she probably needed an upgrade so we should order her a new one. I could tell by the smile on her face that she was satisfied with my help, even if she ended the visit with, "Well, that still won't help me do a print-screen!"

I spent the rest of the day providing high-touch support. Most of the calls were about how-to questions related to features and functions. Fortunately, very few defects were reported. During the development cycle, there was extensive user acceptance testing to validate solid design. There was also lots of learning opportunities for the impacted stakeholders. Yet, it was clear there were plenty of details that still needed reinforcement. It was definitely a full day, but I am happy to say that things stabilized by the end of the week.

Months later, I was talking to Liz in the mailroom when she started asking me questions about the latest technology project I was working on. After I shared some information with her, she shrugged her shoulders and said, "You know, I don't understand why we would need that or how it will help me, but I've learned in the last few months to not worry about it. I've learned not to fear the new stuff because I know you'll take care of us in the end."

As my career progressed and I took on more responsibility in bigger organizations, Liz's words repeatedly echoed in my head. I've learned that when you push really big technology initiatives to people, activating them for change requires comfort-building. However, comfort-building is established in advance of a new system hitting a team member's desk. It comes from a track record of providing consistent, empathetic support, when things don't work as planned. People want timely help from teammates who are kind and demonstrate empathy. While change experts are often employed on projects to smooth the waters for impacted team members who are receiving something new, that work doesn't mean half as much as the established relationship and level of trust built during the last big change.

THE FIRST 30 DAYS

How a project team provides support during the early stages of change is an important tactic for building comfort. Yes, the project team. It's very natural for project team members to think that "Go Live" is the finish line. However, turning the lights on to a new process or system isn't the end; it's the means to an end, which is achieving a new business outcome or capability. Therefore, the work of a project team or change leader shouldn't be considered done until the organization is well-positioned to achieve its goals.

Think back to when you first learned how to ride a bike or swim. You probably had a natural, internal battle of fear and determination. Were your friends already swimming and riding bikes? Most likely, at least a few were. This kept you determined it was possible. It probably also created some urgency because you didn't want to be the odd one out. However, you probably experienced fear and had thoughts like, "What if I'm the one person who breaks an arm because I fell off my bike? What if I'm the one person who drowns in the pool?" Having an encouraging mentor or parent nearby created safety. It reinforced your courage knowing that they could step in if there was an emergency or something didn't go as planned.

Team members often experience the same internal battle of fear and determination when a new change is being implemented at work. They know some of their peers have already learned the new process or system. There's also added pressure from leaders who are communicating an expectation of compliance. Therefore, they are determined, have urgency and don't want to be the odd one out. However, there is typically a counterproductive dose of fear that is also present. It may not be the same kind of fear as drowning or breaking an arm, but it's centered around catastrophic failure, and what the future may or may not hold if they're unsuccessful. This is why leaders need to provide a safety net with a strong support structure, to catch people when they fall.

Since high-touch, personalized support is needed to ultimately get the results we desire, I prefer the project team members themselves provide the help during the early days of a new change. Otherwise, support requests are thrown over the fence to the help desk, who undoubtedly are already providing assistance for lots of other things and who don't have much experience with the new system. It's hard to believe in those situations that team members are going to get the kind of immediate and expert-level support they need to build comfort. This isn't a dig on help desks, it's just reality about what is and isn't possible. Over the years, I've noted it usually takes at least 30 days to stabilize something new. That, of course, is not a hard and fast rule for every organization and change. And I know, some leaders might challenge that keeping project team members allocated to support activities for that amount of time is too expensive. I'd ask, what is the cost of not achieving the change adoption you're expecting?

LONG-TERM SUPPORT INVESTMENTS

Whether it's realistic or not, people have an expectation related to new technology. They expect that it comes with a lifetime warranty! If something isn't working, they want it fixed—now. If something could be enhanced to include added functionality, they want it—now. I've learned through my CIO role, however, that very few companies make an enabling, long-term investment to enhance or support systems in perpetuity or provide that "now" kind of response. As an example, I once worked on a team that implemented over 40 new systems, yet during that same time period didn't add a single additional person to the help desk. That approach clearly impacted the quality of support we provided... which, of course, didn't build stakeholder confidence in future changes.

It took many years of stress and heartache to finally find a remedy for providing good change support. One day, it occurred to me that the business cases I read and authored were mostly focused on the singular event of implementation, while the benefits were expressed and expected in perpetuity. There's an absolute inherent flaw in those assumptions. Software doesn't provide the same benefit in perpetuity without some kind of enhancement along the way. It just doesn't. I know leaders really want it to work that way, but would they expect the same of their car; their house; or even their clothes? It's pretty hard to find an "invest once; enjoy forever" kind of product.

Rather, it is common for organizations and people to have material changes in processes, expectations and/or business environment—which all require significant enhancements to enable. But here's the thing: those unforeseen, needed changes aren't usually covered in the software maintenance upgrades provided by vendors. This is why I started to include the cost of resources needed to wholly support the benefits for the life of the business case in my cost-benefit analysis. While that tactic eroded the value-return of a contemplated change, it more adequately represented what it took to support a desired, long-term outcome. And these investments built the foundation for stronger support experiences, which built credibility and comfort for the future.

When support is an afterthought, it's damaging to an entire organization. It impacts credibility and people's willingness to try new Things. And it certainly makes getting to the top of the awareness-understanding-preference pyramid a near impossibility. Most of us have experienced poor support in our careers and personal lives, and therefore should understand the impact. As an example,

When support is an afterthought, it's
damaging to an entire organization.
It impacts credibility and people's
willingness to try new Things.

have you ever had to contact support for Internet or phone service not working at home? Have you ever interfaced with airline support for lost bags or canceled flights? Has your car required maintenance you thought should be included in the warranty but it wasn't? I'm betting how you were treated in these moments shaped your opinion of the organization you were dealing with. Support is the bread and butter of comfort-building. It satisfies a basic human need and if you can't do that, no one will be interested in trying anything new you have to offer. Plain and simple.

THE PROBLEM IS... CARE

"You give loyalty, you'll get it back.
You give love, you'll get it back."

–Tommy Lasorda

About a year ago, I was traveling out of the San Francisco airport and had the opportunity to try the American Express Centurion Lounge. As a cardholder, I received lots of direct mail pieces advertising the new clubs but hadn't tried one yet. Since I got to the airport early and the club was near my departure gate, I thought, "Why not?" I qualified for free entry and anything had to be better than sitting at a gate designed for 50 people even though at least 150 passengers are waiting for the flight!

As I checked into the lounge, the woman behind the counter asked me if I'd ever visited the club. Since I was a newbie, she carefully shared all the amenities I could enjoy. More on that later.

I was in awe. The facility had beautifully designed aesthetics and limitless free, high quality food and beverage selections. I mean, they were serving Cognac! This felt like one of those "too good to be true" moments. Before I left, I took a survey so I could purely express, "Please don't ever take this amenity away!"

On my way to the crowded gate, I reflected on my last "too good to be true" moment, which happened at the Ritz Carlton in Half Moon Bay. When Kristine and I checked in, we acted like giddy children because of how excited we were; the property was gorgeous! The man behind the counter welcomed us, and then surprised us with a simple and direct question: "Can I offer you a complimentary room upgrade for your visit?" I looked at Kristine and she looked back at me as if we were just asked a trick question. Simultaneously we said, "Yeeeaah, we'd love one!" He topped off the check-in process by asking, "Can I offer the two of you a glass of wine?" Now we were really pinching ourselves.

It's natural to read these stories and jump to the conclusion, "Duh! These amenities are all benefits that result from being a premium American Express customer and a guest at the Ritz Carlton." However, I saved the punch line for you. Remember the woman behind the counter at the American Express lounge? That's where the truly special and magical part of the experience happened.

As soon as she heard I was a first-time guest, she was beaming with pride to curate my visit. She was so kind and patiently walked me through all the options I should explore, even though she delivers that spiel hundreds of times a day. Honestly, I felt like a guest in her home.

The same was 100% true at the Ritz. And it didn't end with the man behind the counter. Every team member we encountered was just as insanely nice and helpful—from the restaurant servers to the bartenders to housekeepers to groundskeepers.

There are many ways to explain those experiences. Since I've been an executive in the hospitality space, I couldn't help but consider the options. It is easy to believe what I experienced was a product of brand standards and good training. After all, I've heard plenty of people say, "I don't understand why I'm getting such poor service. It's just not that hard!" This type of statement implies that it shouldn't be hard to have a standard for good service and for team members to know and follow those standards.

But to me, the problem isn't... hard. I believe a lot of companies do have standards that address service. And I don't believe their team members have difficulty remembering the standards or deliberately choose to ignore what's expected of them.

No, I think the problem is... care. If you want customers to love your brand, it starts with your team members loving your brand. And I know love is a strong word, but without it, there would be no motive for passion. As an example, you could give a newly married couple a contract of expectations (think standards) that outlines all the musts and must-nots of the relationship. However, if there isn't an authentic love between the individuals, the rules will likely get broken and the relationship will be compromised.

The same is true with a company and its customers. Team members who authentically love a brand will create customers who love a brand. Team members who

If you want customers to love
your brand, it starts with your team
members loving your brand.

like a brand will only create customers who like a brand. And, team members who hate a brand will certainly lose customers who grow to hate that brand.

I think the same could inherently be said about an individual's work with internal stakeholders, too. Despite whether or not you are good at your craft, people will notice if you love, like, or hate your department or team. It's hard to hide a state of like or hate with solid work quality alone because stakeholders don't just judge the things you produce—they also judge how you treat people in the process.

So, if the problem is care, how do leaders get their team members to care? Unfortunately, there's no universal answer to this question. But if you're a leader, I would ask: what would it take for you to love the organization you serve? Certainly, you wouldn't expect your team members to love an organization you don't love. If you do love where you work, is it possible for your team members to love it for the same reasons? If so, evangelize those reasons!

After reading this book, I hope you conclude a good start is to put People Before Things. Human connection and experience provide a path to meaning, hope, and authenticity. A well-respected mentor once told me, "People walk around with an invisible sign on their foreheads that says *"Make Me Feel Important."* It's a leader's job to make their people feel important, nurtured, and supported, which will grow the kind of authentic love that shines through to other stakeholders and customers. Doesn't that sound like a win-win?

Whether it's an enlightened vision, a big change initiative, a set of milestones, or a daily task list, the Things can't be all leaders think and talk about. Good ideas don't transform organizations and results—People do. So go forth and lead with your heart; change your organization; show your team members you care and; finally, always put People Before Things! Always!

THE NITTY GRITTY

"It's the little details that are vital.
Little things make big things happen."

—John Wooden

WHAT'S THE POINT?

We all read business books differently. Some folks like audio books; some prefer cliff notes and cheat sheets, and; yet others enjoy the 500-page variety of academic reading. One thing is clear—a "one-size fits all" approach rarely works.

As such, I toiled in the writing process of this book. I wanted to find the perfect balance between presenting high-level concepts (ones that don't prescribe solutions) and providing enough detail so readers can successfully implement these ideas.

In the end, I decided the right thing to do was to include an appendix of resources that provide the nitty gritty details. This approach ensures people who prefer high-level reading can be exposed to the conditions of change leadership without getting lost in execution notes. However, if you're looking for a little more "meat on the bones" about any one condition outlined in the book, you've come to the right place.

I'm a big believer in leveraging tried and true strategies and tactics; it doesn't make sense to develop a new technique when something effective already exists. Therefore, in most cases, I will simply direct you to a diverse group of respected thought leaders so you can explore on your own. While I'm a pretty picky chooser of business books, I've grown my library quite a bit these days with many of the authors I reference, and I enthusiastically encourage you to do the same.

ALIGNMENT

Establishing true alignment is tough. However, the teams who are most aligned can accomplish the unthinkable. I find the two biggest blockers to alignment are: 1) A team is not operating cohesively and therefore cannot nurture a healthy, functional organization or; 2) A cohesively operating team doesn't have a strong template for how to debate critical topics and rally around a common objective.

For a team not operating cohesively, it takes a courageous leader to bring attention to the matter. I had an executive coach recommend an effective and non-intimidating way to broach the subject: ask your teammates, "Is it just me or does it seem like we're not on the same page right now?" This tactic brings light to the dysfunctions of the organization but doesn't explicitly point the finger, which my coach referred to as, "throwing stones."

If the team mostly agrees with you, I would seek knowledge from Patrick Lencioni's books, *The Advantage* and *Five Dysfunctions of a Team* to help build organizational health. He also has a boutique consulting firm called *The Table Group*. If you go to **www.tablegroup.com**, there are all kinds of resources that help you diagnose an unhealthy team and identify a solution path that will make your team stronger. As Pat would say, "It's a messy and complicated process," but I really believe his advice and approach is very practical.

And let me just reiterate that, if you are having organizational health issues, you should stop everything else you're doing and focus on it. Attempting to drive large-scale, disruptive change when there is dysfunction on a leadership team is setting your organization up for disaster!

If you believe you're on a cohesive team but would like to explore a method for facilitating debates that lead to productive outcomes, I really like Edward de Bono's book, *Six Thinking Hats*. I use this framework in cross-functional meetings that are focused on controversial or hard-to-mediate topics. You can practically read the book in one sitting, and it's very easy to share the techniques with a room full of people who haven't read it. In summary, Edward de Bono points out that in Western culture, we tend to make a point, and someone else presents a counterpoint. Then, we present a counterpoint to the counterpoint. This style isn't productive. So, Edward explores a method inspired by Eastern culture that has the whole team looking at the positives, negatives, risks, etc., at the same time.

DESIGN

The design chapter of this book focuses on the role leaders play to keep their teams disciplined about the solutions they are creating. When a solution is tightly aligned to the underlying WHY of a business challenge or opportunity (and nothing more), unnecessary complexities are avoided. The discussion stayed at a high level and focused on human-centered design, maintaining a "less is more" discipline, and always communicating to impacted stakeholders what's next in the future roadmap.

However, if you would like to dig deeper on how to ensure simple, easy-to-use (internal or external) products are delivered through your teams, I believe that *Hooked* by Nir Eyal provides a practical approach to design. In Nir's model, he explores the interplay of Triggers, Actions, and Rewards in driving human behavior and building the habits you need stakeholders to adopt to achieve your expected outcome(s). His philosophy is that simple design always trumps motivation tactics designed to coerce people into accepting new Things. Obviously, I couldn't agree more.

CAPACITY

I'm an ardent believer in the "Vital Few," which comes from the Pareto Principle: 80% of the return will come from 20% of the effort. While this belief has caused a lot of conflict for me throughout my executive career, I'm certain it was responsible for many of my successes. I think leaders and individuals will gain a lot when they take inventory of their life and work and purge all unnecessary activities. The best book I've read on the topic is *Essentialism* by Greg McKeown. I've also had the great privilege of listening to him speak twice. He is a master at explaining the WHY behind a "disciplined pursuit of less."

In my opinion, the second best technique to Vital Few leadership is to have a strong understanding of your organization's capacity. As I mentioned in the Capacity chapter, time and motion studies and the exact science of industrial engineering provide invaluable insights about the effort required to do a work task or absorb change. That said, many leaders don't invest the dollars or time to do them.

In lieu of industrial engineering work, leaders can perform an easy and high-level analysis of the incremental effort required by a new change initiative. I call this the **Capacity Index**. Part of the Capacity Index analysis is a no brainer and part of it is the secret sauce. (Isn't that always the case?)

The straightforward part looks at the time required by an individual team member to adapt to a new change. That time should be multiplied by the number of team members that are impacted. The secret sauce is to include an inflator that is based on the collective organization's experience with such a change. I like to use an inflator of 1 for changes an organization is used to and routinely performs, a 3 for things that are rarely done and don't fit into the core business or day-to-day activities, and a 2 for things that fall in the middle. Let me give you an example that includes two different kinds of changes and leverages case studies from

Red Robin:

Change #1 is a promotional menu item that will run for a few weeks in all restaurants. It will take certain team members in a given restaurant (cooks and servers) approximately one hour to learn how to prepare and serve the new item. Promotional menu items are pretty common in the restaurant business and team members are accustomed to learning and serving them. Here's what it looks like in a calculation:

> ## 35 Team Members (cooks, servers)
> ## x 1 Hour x 1 (Inflator based on experience) =
> ## Capacity Index of 35

Change #2 is the implementation of a new time and attendance system that will impact all 50 hourly team members in the restaurant. To be successful, people will need to learn about new clock-in/clock-out procedures, the rules for reporting breaks, and the process for approving and submitting their timecards. This will require one hour of training. However, most servers, bussers, hosts, and cooks don't use technology in their day-to-day jobs and the managers in the restaurant aren't used to receiving IT-related training. Here's what this calculation looks like:

> 50 Team Members (servers, bussers, hosts, cooks)
> **X** 1 hour **X** 3 (Inflator based on experience) =
> Capacity Index of 150

The least important part of the Capacity Index is the calculation itself—you can change it if you'd like, but just ensure it's consistent across all change initiatives. The most important part of the Capacity Index is the relative weighting of one initiative against another. So, in the examples above, it's clear that Change #2, the new time and attendance system, will have a much greater impact on the restaurant than Change #1, the new promotional menu item. The Capacity Index in this example makes it easy for any audience of leaders to understand the comparison of these changes. After all, Change #2 had a score of 150 and Change #1 has a score of 35. Therefore, it stands to reason the restaurants will need more time to absorb and fully adapt to Change #2.

A given leader may only be responsible for pushing one or two major changes throughout the course of a year. However, the impacted team members may be receiving dozens of changes during the same period of time. Having a macro view of those changes and being able to provide a monthly Capacity Index roll-up will help leaders prepare for the times of year which may be more heavily weighted with change than others. Said another way, when implementing a new Thing that is VITAL to the business, it may make sense to clear the decks of other new Things to ensure the total team is doing a great job with the vital one.

I will say it again—this doesn't have to be an all or none proposition. Therefore, if Change #1 requires 35 hours to learn and implement, it doesn't mean you have to necessarily find 35 hours of time-savings to be successful. However, the closer you get to offsetting the time and effort required to take on a new change, the more likely you will achieve your expected outcome(s).

COMMUNICATIONS

As I've said in the book and many of my blogs, the power of communications is often overplayed. Therefore, I'm not pointing to many resources to round out this subject. However, I'd like to highlight a method, which I believe is highly effective, especially in larger organizations—video updates.

A common tactic used in communication is think-analyze-change. As an example, in a written memo or PowerPoint presentation, we may outline key data and hope our audience will *analyze* this information, which will change the way they think, ultimately leading to behavior change. Our desire is for them to take action and do what we want them to do. Unfortunately, while analytics may provide rational reasoning to do something, people are mostly irrational beings. I believe a better tactic is see-feel-change. We want people to see something, which makes them feel something and this feeling will prompt them to do something. I learned about this cycle from a short video clip Dan Heath produced called, *Want Your Organization to Change? Put Feelings First* and can be found on YouTube. (You should also pick up a copy of his book, *Switch*.)

In situations when it isn't practical to meet with people in town halls or face-to-face meetings, I strongly encourage leaders to produce videos so their audience can see something. When you consider the age of selfie videos, it doesn't even require high-production costs to be successful. These videos will provide people with more context and tone than a memo ever could. Also, videos give leaders the opportunity to do storytelling and connect people to purpose (the WHY) behind a given change.

LEARNING

There's a book I like called *Analyzing Performance Problems: Or, You Really Oughta Wanna* by Robert Mager and Peter Pipe. One of the outcomes of this book is a fundamental understanding about when learning should be used as a solution to a performance problem. So while I outlined the "gun to the head" litmus test in the Learning chapter, this book includes a detailed flow chart that points to all the issues that may be blocking performance. As an example, the flow chart asks if people are being punished for performance. This planned or unplanned punishment is what's really blocking changes in behavior or improvement in performance. Bottom line: we shouldn't always conclude people need to learn more to perform better. There may be other blockers causing poor performance and non-compliance.

STAKEHOLDER ENGAGEMENT

I wholeheartedly believe in grassroots leadership. The people closest to the action often have the strongest ideas about solutions for everyday problems blocking team members and customers from memorable experiences. I also believe social collaboration and networking provides an unprecedented opportunity to build community within the grassroots. Charlene Li offers two books, which are practical guides on how leaders can leverage the power of social networks: *Open Leadership* and *The Engaged Leader*. Admittedly, Charlene makes small mention of the work I participated in during my tenure at Red Robin, but honestly, I would have recommended these books anyway!

SUPPORT

Not much to say here because it's all about execution and empathy. However, here are some simple suggestions for project teams to provide good support during a change transition: first, provide a regularly scheduled conference call (perhaps daily) after a new change goes live that is optional for people to call in and ask questions. Next, ensure there is solid corporate listening across multiple channels such as social networks and town hall meetings. Finally, keep frequently asked questions in a published document that is current. It's important with all of these methods to *publicly highlight* problems, as well as the solutions. This will normalize the situation for everyone involved and reinforce if something doesn't go as planned, support is close by.

ACKNOWLEDGMENTS

Admittedly, until I went through the process of writing a book, I mostly ignored the Acknowledgments of other authors. If I ask myself, "Why," it's mostly because it's hard to connect to a list of names you don't know—especially with no context for why they were being thanked. Therefore, I want to do more here. I want to mention some important influences, without whom this book would have never been written.

First and foremost, to my business and life partner, Kristine Gail Porter. I'm so blessed to have you in my life. We had many, many conversations about putting your name on the cover, but you wouldn't let me. The readers need to know that your rewrites, developmental editing, people philosophies, and practical solutions greatly shaped this book. The second half of 2015 will forever live in my heart as the most fun I've had in my career because of your partnership and contributions!

I'd like to thank some good friends who inspired and supported the journey to publish *People Before Things*. Chris and Jen Smaldone, thank you for letting us "borrow" the label for your family value of People Before Things; Jeff and Meg Henrickson, for encouraging us to stop "working for the man" and to create something we could own; Jason Rapert, for providing creative direction (you have mad skills) for the book and website and; Gai Swanson, for not only being a close friend and awesome former landlord but agreeing to provide copy editing.

To Vicki and Steve Musselman, I'm so lucky to have a sister- and brother-in-law who support my faith and writing like you do. Your recommendation to read *The Little Red Book of Wisdom* was the final push I needed to follow my passions. That book helped me truly understand how mixing professional and personal beliefs can be beautifully transformative to yourself and the people you work with.

To my family, thank you for always believing in me. Whenever I shared crazy ideas and all of my business pursuits, you smiled and reiterated I could do anything I put my mind to. And to my parents and in-laws—even at 43 years-old, I still need your belief like a child.

To the team at Red Robin, you can't work somewhere for eight years and not call your teammates family. I'm so grateful to all of you and incredibly proud of everything you've accomplished! It was such an important time in my life and career, and I couldn't have asked for a better experience.

To my all my friends at Trace3 and PoPin, I couldn't ask for a warmer support blanket! You are a selfless bunch who have always been good friends and business partners. You introduced me to Patrick Lencioni, who in one single afternoon forever changed the way I viewed leadership.

Finally, I want to thank God. His Son's life on this planet was the most authentic demonstration of what it means to always put People Before Things.

PEOPLE BEFORE THINGS

So, you've read the book and want more? People Before Things coaches leaders and organizations on the conditions needed to enable and activate people for change.

SPEAKING

For the past 10 years and from his CIO post, Chris Laping has been engaging audiences throughout the U.S. with disruptive ideas on innovation and roller-coaster storytelling. Now, he is hitting the stage as Author and CEO/Co-Founder of People Before Things to take you on a journey that focuses on how great organizations inspire a culture of change. Whether it's a large audience at a national conference or a small, private group at a corporate event, Chris brings the same level of energy to each talk—and with content that's tailored for each unique audience!

LEADERSHIP DEVELOPMENT

Nothing is more impactful than a cohesive team that is aligned on what's important and how THINGS will get accomplished. At facilitated offsites, we coach executive and IT leadership teams on the conditions needed to enable and activate PEOPLE for change—while integrating their organization's unique culture, strategy, business problems and projects.

Our goal is to grow your team's change leadership skills, allowing you to think about and deliver change as a cohesive team. By using the offsite as a forum to discuss and debate an upcoming or contemplated change, such as a large-scale IT implementation, we can leave you with a tangible action plan.

We also offer change leadership coaching on an individual, on-going basis. This model maps personal development goals to tangible action plans, allowing any executive or IT leader to grow into an effective CHANGE leader.

www.peoplebeforethings.co
info@peoplebeforethings.co
720.663.9162

NOTES

NOTES

NOTES

NOTES